T0295611

CONTEMPORARY ISSUES IN FINANCIAL ECONOMICS

RESEARCH IN FINANCE

Series Editor: Rita Biswas

Recent Volumes:

Volumes 6–25:   Edited by Andrew H. Chen
Volumes 26–34:   Edited by John W. Kensinger
Volumes 35 and 36:   Edited by Rita Biswas and Michael Michaelides

RESEARCH IN FINANCE   VOLUME 37

CONTEMPORARY ISSUES IN FINANCIAL ECONOMICS: EVIDENCE FROM EMERGING ECONOMIES

EDITED BY

RITA BISWAS
University at Albany, USA

AND

MICHAEL MICHAELIDES
Allegheny College, USA

United Kingdom – North America – Japan
India – Malaysia – China

Emerald Publishing Limited
Howard House, Wagon Lane, Bingley BD16 1WA, UK

First edition 2023

Reprints and permissions service
Contact: www.copyright.com

British Library Cataloguing in Publication Data
A catalogue record for this book is available from the British Library

ISBN: 978-1-80117-839-6 (Print)
ISBN: 978-1-80117-838-9 (Online)
ISBN: 978-1-80117-840-2 (Epub)

ISSN: 0196-3821 (Series)

INVESTOR IN PEOPLE

CONTENTS

LIST OF CONTRIBUTORS

Desi Adhariani	Universitas Indonesia, Indonesia
Naufal Daffaveda Adam	Deutsche Bank, Indonesia
Frista	Universitas Kristen Duta Wacana, Indonesia
Amlan Ghosh	National Institute of Technology, India
Ancella Anitawati Hermawan	Universitas Indonesia, Indonesia
Robin Lieb	International School of Management, Germany.
Refin Dimas Pratama	Universitas Indonesia, Indonesia
Malisa Salsabila	Universitas Indonesia, Indonesia
Sylvia Veronica Siregar	Universitas Indonesia, Indonesia
Sidharta Utama	Universitas Indonesia, Indonesia
Rama Sastry Vinjamury	Narsee Monjee Institute of Management Studies, India

INTRODUCTION

This volume focuses on contemporary issues in financial economics spanning from board diversity to sustainable finance. The first chapter focuses on the impact of board gender diversity on dividend payout decisions in India. This is followed by a study examining the benefits of early adoption of sustainable finance by government-owned banks in Indonesia. Next, a cross-country study analyzes the influences of country-level as well as firm-level governance quality on the adoption of sustainable finance in the banking sector. Following this, we present a chapter that examines the relation between financial market freedom and economic growth in India followed by another cross-country study examining the relation between labor rights and equity market performance. The final chapters are related to Indonesia – one study examines the impact of adopting eXtensible Business Reporting Language (XBRL) on earnings management while the final chapter explores the relation between financial slack and green banking activities.

CHAPTER 1

CORPORATE BOARD GENDER DIVERSITY AND DIVIDEND DECISIONS: EVIDENCE FROM INDIA

Rama Sastry Vinjamury

ABSTRACT

The Indian Companies Act (2013) mandates the appointment of at least one woman director for large publicly listed companies in India in order to increase gender diversity on corporate boards. The study analyzes the relationship between corporate governance mechanisms, board gender diversity, and ownership structure on dividend payout decisions in an emerging economy like India. The study uses data collected for nonfinancial firms listed on NSE (National Stock Exchange) 500 in India from the period 2008 to 2020. Contrary to the evidence from developed economies, the study finds that increased female representation and greater proportion of female independent directors on the board are associated with lower dividend payout decisions in the Indian context. As it stands, the female representation on corporate boards in India is woefully low and appears to be mere tokenism. The study explores the role of regulation in increasing gender diversity on corporate boards and offers insights from an emerging economy where such a regulation is in place.

Keywords: Corporate governance; gender diversity; ownership structure; dividend decisions; India; board of directors

Contemporary Issues in Financial Economics: Evidence from Emerging Economies
Research in Finance, Volume 37, 1–13
Copyright © 2023 by Emerald Publishing Limited
All rights of reproduction in any form reserved
ISSN: 0196-3821/doi:10.1108/S0196-382120230000037001

1. INTRODUCTION

Corporate governance can be viewed as a set of mechanisms by which the "suppliers of finance to corporations assure themselves of getting a return on their investment" (Shlifer & Vishny, 1997). Corporate governance encompasses mechanisms that allow stakeholders of a corporation to exercise control over firm insiders and management so that their interests are protected (John & Senbet, 1998). In other words, corporate governance mechanisms may help address the issue of separation of ownership and control, which can often lead to agency problems. In this context, dividend policy can be viewed as a corporate governance device. Specifically, dividend policy can be viewed as a means to mitigate Jensen's (1986) free cash flow problem. In a similar vein, prior studies posit that dividends reduce the free cash within the firm, thereby reducing the agency costs (e.g., Easterbrook, 1984; Rozeff, 1982).

Given the importance of corporate governance, developing economies such as India have introduced regulatory changes to strengthen corporate governance mechanisms. For example, the Companies Act (2013) enacted by the Parliament of India seeks for a major overhaul of corporate governance norms to be adopted by firms in India. Also, Securities and Exchange Board of India (SEBI) introduced revised Clause 49, where requirements for firms have been changed to bring it in line with the Companies Act (2013). Not surprisingly, the key provisions of the Act pertain to board composition. For example, Section 149 (1) of the Indian Companies Act (2013) provides for compulsory appointment of at least one woman director for large publicly listed companies in India. Introduction of such a provision may be viewed in light of the emerging literature, which analyzes the impact of female directors and managers on corporate decision-making. This literature suggests that female directors and managers have a significant impact on these decisions. For example, Matsa and Miller (2013) show that female directors are less likely to downsize the workforce. Similarly, female directors are less likely to make acquisition bids and are more likely to make acquisitions with lower bid premiums (Levi, Li, & Zhang, 2014). Also, female directors take on less debt and are more likely to make less risky financing and investment choices (Faccio, Marchica, & Mura, 2016).

Firm's dividend policy is an important corporate decision deliberated by the board. In this context, recent studies have analyzed the role of female board members on dividend decisions in developed economies (e.g., Chen, Leung, & Goergen, 2017). Adams and Ferreira (2009) and Chen et al. (2017) provide empirical evidence that female directors focus more on monitoring than their male counterparts on corporate boards. In this context, dividend decisions can be viewed in terms of the monitoring role performed by female board members. Specifically, dividend policy can be viewed as a mechanism to mitigate Jensen's (1986) free cash flow problem. Dividends may reduce the free cash within the firm and may contribute toward reducing the agency costs (e.g., Easterbrook, 1984; Rozeff, 1982). This argument assumes that a high dividend payout might compel the firm to return to the capital markets frequently to meet their funding needs and attracts greater scrutiny from the market participants. However, most of these studies are focused on developed economies and there is a gap in analyzing the role of female directors on dividend decisions for firms in emerging economies.

Given this background, this chapter attempts to analyze the role of female directors on corporate boards as monitors in mitigating agency problems. Prior studies (e.g., Chen et al., 2017) argue that dividend payouts can be viewed as a monitoring device and larger payouts can be viewed as a means to reduce free cash flow and related agency problems. In view of such a link between monitoring and dividend payouts, the study analyzes the relationship between presence of female directors on the board and the propensity to pay dividends. Contrary to the evidence provided by Chen et al. (2017), this study finds that the presence of female directors on boards in an emerging economy such as India is associated with lower dividend payouts to its shareholders. This result is statistically significant and holds true for the presence of independent female directors on the board. Consistent with previous studies (e.g., Chen et al., 2017; Hu & Kumar, 2004), the study finds that propensity to pay dividends is positively associated with increase in board size and board independence. Also, greater audit committee independence is positively associated with dividend payouts. In addition, the study finds that the propensity to pay dividends is negatively associated with greater promoter ownership. On the other hand, dividend payouts are positively associated with the increase in *pressure-sensitive* institutional investors.

The rest of the chapter is organized as follows: Section 2 discusses Companies Act (2013) enacted by the Indian Parliament and the role of women directors as per the Act. Section 3 provides a literature review and lists objectives of the study. Section 4 discusses data and methodology adopted for the study. Section 5 discusses empirical results. Section 6 discusses policy implications and conclusions.

2. THE COMPANIES ACT (2013) AND WOMEN DIRECTORS

The Companies Act (2013) is an Act[1] of the Parliament of India. The Act among other things regulates the incorporation, responsibilities, and dissolution of a company in its jurisdiction. Among other provisions, the Act aims to introduce major corporate governance reforms to be adopted by firms in India. Many provisions of the Act pertain to corporate board composition. For example, the Act stipulates that:

> every company shall have a Board of Directors consisting of individuals as directors and shall have
>
> (a) a minimum number of three directors in the case of a public company, two directors in the case of a private company, and one director in the case of a one-person company; and
> (b) a maximum of fifteen directors.[2]

Also, "every listed public company shall have at least one-third of the total number of directors as independent directors." Of special interest to this study is Section 149 (1) of the Act, which provides for compulsory appointment of at least one woman director for large publicly listed companies in India. As per the Act, the following class of companies shall appoint at least one-woman director

(i)   every listed company;
(ii)   every other public company having—
       (a)   paid-up share capital of one hundred crore rupees or more; or
       (b)   turnover of three hundred crore rupees or more.

Given that the appointment of at least one woman director on a listed company board is mandatory (the study is focusing on listed companies), the study attempts to analyze the impact of such a regulation on corporate decision in terms of dividend payouts.

3. LITERATURE REVIEW AND OBJECTIVES OF THE STUDY

Many studies in the recent past in developed economies have focused their attention on analyzing the impact of female board members on firm value, performance, and risk-taking behavior (e.g., Ahern & Dittmar, 2012; Dezso & Ross, 2012; Faccio et al., 2016; Matsa & Miller, 2013). Specifically, Faccio et al. (2016) show that female directors are less likely to take on debt and are more likely to make less risky financing and investment choices. In addition, other studies have analyzed the role of female directors in influencing corporate decisions. For example, Levi et al. (2014) show that female directors are less likely to make acquisition bids. In case of an acquisition bid, female directors tend to make acquisitions with lower bid premiums. In a similar vein, Miller and Triana (2009) report that propensity to spend more on research and development increases with female directors on the board.

There is a growing body of literature that suggests that the discussions of complex decision problems improve when female directors are part of the decision-making processes (e.g., Gul, Srinidhi, & Ng, 2011). In addition, Adams and Ferreira (2009) and Chen et al. (2017) find that female directors are more likely to engage in monitoring and provide empirical evidence that female directors focus more on monitoring than their male counterparts on corporate boards.

To analyze the monitoring role of female directors on the board, prior studies have looked at firm's dividend policy (e.g., Chen et al., 2017). In this context, dividend policy can be viewed as a mechanism to mitigate Jensen's (1986) free cash flow problem. Prior studies argue that dividends reduce the free cash within the firm which helps in reducing the agency costs (e.g., Easterbrook, 1984; Rozeff, 1982). Specifically, Easterbrook (1984) argues that dividend plays a corporate governance role. This argument assumes that a high dividend payout might compel the firm to return to the capital markets frequently to meet their funding needs and attracts greater scrutiny from the market participants.

Brickley, Lease, and Smith (1988) provide a model where they categorize institutional investors as pressure-sensitive or pressure-insensitive institutional investors. They posit that pressure-insensitive institutional investors are more likely to monitor and discipline the managers. On the other hand, pressure-sensitive institutional investors are likely to have existing business relationships with the firm and are less likely to be effective monitors. Consistent with this view, studies (e.g., Almazan, Hartzell, & Starks, 2005) show that institutional ownership is negatively associated with the level of executive compensation and the relationship is stronger for pressure-sensitive institutional investors. Also, Cornett, Marcus, Saunders, and Tehranian (2007) document a positive relationship between pressure-insensitive institutional investors and corporate operating performance. At the same time, the presence of pressure-sensitive institutional investors has no impact on a firm's operating cash flow returns.

Given this background, the objective of the study is to understand the role of corporate governance mechanisms, board gender diversity, and ownership structure on dividend payout decisions in an emerging economy like India. Specifically,

(1) to analyze the relationship between board gender diversity and firm's propensity to pay dividends in an emerging economy like India; and
(2) to analyze the role of firm ownership structure on dividend decisions. Specifically, how increased promoter ownership and presence of pressure-sensitive and pressure-resistant institutional investors impacts dividend decisions.

4. DATA AND METHODOLOGY

The data for the study are from the Centre for Monitoring Indian Economy (CMIE) Prowess database. Data were collected for nonfinancial firms listed on the National Stock Exchange (NSE) 500 in India for the period 2008–2020.

The dependent variable used for the analysis is dividend payout (DIV_PAYOUT), which is a binary variable. DIV_PAYOUT takes on a value of "1" in the event of a dividend payment and "0" otherwise. Logit models are used given the nature of the data used for the analysis. To determine the role of female directors, other corporate governance variables and ownership structure on dividend payout decisions, the following baseline model is considered.

$$
\begin{aligned}
DIV\_PAYOUT_{it} = {} & \alpha_0 + \beta Board\ gender\ diversity_{it} \\
& + \delta Other\ governance\ variables_{it} \\
& + \gamma Ownership\ variables_{it} + \theta Control\ variables_{it} \\
& + Industry_i + Year_t + \varepsilon_{it}
\end{aligned} \tag{1}
$$

In addition to the logit model described above, a panel tobit regression model with year and industry fixed effects is also employed. Tobit_DIV_PAYOUT$_{it}$ is used as a dependent variable for the tobit model. This variable represents the ratio of dividends to total net income. Since dividends cannot be negative, the dependent variable is left censored. Therefore, the tobit model is specified as follows:

$$
\begin{aligned}
Tobit\_DIV\_PAYOUT_{it} = {} & \alpha_0 + \beta Board\ gender\ diversity_{it} \\
& + \delta Other\ governance\ variables_{it} \\
& + \gamma Ownership\ variables_{it} + \theta Control\ variables_{it} \\
& + Industry_i + Year_t + \varepsilon_{it}
\end{aligned} \tag{2a}
$$

where $Tobit\_DIV\_PAYOUT_{it} > 0$

$$\text{Tobit}\_\text{DIV}\_\text{PAYOUT}_{it} = 0, \text{where Tobit}\_\text{DIV}\_\text{PAYOUT}_{it} \leq 0 \quad (2b)$$

The models (logit and tobit) specified above do not lend themselves to causal inference, but allow us to analyze the associations between dependent and independent variables. For more detailed analysis, four models each for logit and tobit models are considered in this study (i.e., a total of eight models). In the first and fifth models, the impact of female directors on dividend payout decisions is analyzed. In the second and sixth models, proportion of independent female directors is included for the analysis. In the third, fourth, seventh, and eighth models, in addition to the role of gender diversity, the role of pressure-sensitive and pressure-resistant institutional shareholders on dividend payout decisions is analyzed.

In terms of board gender diversity, the proportion of female directors on the board (B_FEMALE) and independent female directors on the board (FEMALE_IND) are considered. Other corporate governance variables used in the analysis are board size (BSIZE), board independence (BIND), audit committee independence (AIND), number of board meetings (BMEETINGS) (e.g., see Vinjamury, 2020). In terms of ownership variables, promoter ownership (PROMOTERS), pressure-sensitive institutional investor ownership (P_SENSITIVE) and pressure-resistant institutional investor ownership (P_RESISTANT) are considered for the analysis along with other control variables.

LOG_TA represents natural logarithm of firm total assets and is used as a proxy for firm size. Leverage (LEVERAGE) is defined as the ratio of total borrowings to total assets. Adjusted Tobin's Q (TQ) is used as a proxy for growth opportunities. TQ was obtained using similar calculations as in Gompers, Ishii, and Metrick (2003). Following Chen et al. (2017), ratio of cash holding to net fixed assets is used as a measure of liquidity (LIQUIDITY). Return on Assets (ROA) is used as a measure for profitability. Other factors constant, more profitable companies may have a propensity to pay higher dividends. Again following Chen et al. (2017), ratio of net fixed assets to total assets (ASSET_TANGIBILITY) and ratio of research and development to sales (RD_SALES) are used as a proxy for asset tangibility and financial distress costs.

In terms of other governance characteristics, board size (BSIZE) and percentage of independent directors (BIND) are used as control variables. Audit committee independence (AIND) and frequency of board meetings (BMEETINGS) are used to capture the extent of monitoring by the board members. Finally, FAGE is used to control for the age of the firm. The construction of these variables for empirical analysis is described in Table 1.1. Both industry fixed effects and year fixed effects are accounted for in the analysis.

Table 1.2 reports summary statistics of the variables used in the study. The median dividend payout ratio (DIV_PAYOUT) for the sample firms is close to 22%. The median board size (BSIZE) of the firms used in the analysis is 11. The median board independence (BIND) is 50%. The mean and median promoter institutional shareholdings (PROMOTER) are 55.57% and 55.44%, respectively. Of the total institutional ownership, the mean pressure-sensitive (P_SENSITIVE) and pressure-insensitive (P_RESISTANT) institutional ownership represents 4.078% and 10.816%, respectively. The median audit committee independence (AIND) for the sample firms is 75%. The mean proportion of female board

Table 1.1. Description of the Variables Used in the Study.

Variable	Description	How Is it Measured
TQ	Adjusted Tobin's Q	(Total assets + market capitalization – book value of equity – deferred tax liability)/total assets
ROA	Return on assets	Net income/total assets
DIV_PAYOUT	Dividend payouts	Ratio of dividends to net income. Is a binary variable, Defined as "1" in case of dividend payment and "0" otherwise
BSIZE	Board size	Number of directors on the board
BIND	Board independence	Number of independent directors on board/ number of directors on board
BMEETINGS	Board meetings	Frequency of annual board meetings
AIND	Audit committee independence	Percentage of independent directors on the audit committee
B_FEMALE	Female directors	Number of female directors on the board
FEMALE_IND	Female independent directors	Number of female independent directors on the board
PROMOTERS	Promoter shareholdings	Percentage of shares held by the promoters
P_INSENSITIVE	Pressure insensitive institutional investors	Percentage of shares held by nonpromoter mutual funds and foreign institutional investors
P_SENSITIVE	Pressure sensitive institutional investors	Percentage of shares held by nonpromoter banks and financial institutions
FAGE	Firm's age	Age of the firm since its incorporation (in years)
LEVERAGE	Leverage	Ratio of total borrowings to total assets
RD_SALES	R&D expenses to sales	Ratio of research and development to sales
LIQUIDITY	Liquid assets	Ratio of cash to net fixed assets
TANGIBLE_ASSETS	Tangible assets	Ratio of net fixed assets to total assets
LOG_TA	Logarithm of total assets	Natural log of total assets

Note: The table describes the variables used in the study.

Table 1.2. Descriptive Statistics.

Variable	N	Mean	Median
DIV_PAYOUT	3,919	0.214	0.219
BSIZE	3,919	11.742	11.000
BIND	3,919	0.502	0.500
B_FEMALE	3,919	0.044	0.000
FEMALE_IND	3,919	0.026	0.000
AIND	3,919	0.720	0.750
BMEETINGS	3,919	4.377	4.000
FAGE	3,919	40.730	33.000
LOG_ASSETS	3,919	10.223	10.152
TANGIBLE_ASSETS	3,919	0.276	0.260
LIQUIDITY	3,919	0.013	0.001
RD_SALES	3,919	0.017	0.001
LEVERAGE	3,919	0.177	0.134
ROA	3,919	0.088	0.080
TQ	3,919	2.833	1.998
P_SENSITIVE	3,919	4.078	1.690
P_RESISTANT	3,919	10.816	8.570
PROMOTERS	3,919	55.570	55.440

Note: The table reports the number of observations (N), mean (Mean), and median (Median) of the variables used in the study. Refer to Table 1.1 for a detailed description of the variables.

Table 1.3. Correlation Matrix.

	DIV_PAYOUT	BSIZE	BIND	B_FEMALE	FEMALE_IND	AIND	BMEETINGS	FAGE	LOG_ASSETS	TANGIBLE_ASSETS	LIQUIDITY	RD_SALES	LEVERAGE	ROA	TQ	P_SENSITIVE	P_RESISTANT	PROMOTERS
DIV_PAYOUT	1																	
BSIZE	-0.02	1																
BIND	0	-0.11	1															
B_FEMALE	0.01	0.04	0.03	1														
FEMALE_IND	0.01	0.04	0.11	0.72	1													
AIND	-0.01	-0.02	0.27	-0.08	-0.08	1												
BMEETINGS	0.01	-0.42	0.01	-0.1	-0.09	0.07	1											
FAGE	-0.02	0.13	0.02	0	-0.01	0.17	-0.04	1										
LOG_ASSETS	-0.01	0.4	-0.02	0.08	0.09	0.04	0	0.18	1									
TANGIBLE_ASSETS	0.01	0.05	0.06	-0.02	-0.03	0.04	0.02	-0.05	0.04	1								
LIQUIDITY	0	-0.01	-0.01	0	0.02	0	0.02	0.01	0.01	-0.09	1							
RD_SALES	0	-0.03	0.02	0.02	0.05	0.03	-0.03	-0.06	-0.07	0.02	-0.01	1						
LEVERAGE	-0.02	0.01	0.05	-0.07	-0.08	0.04	0.07	-0.05	0.13	0.44	-0.05	-0.31	1					
ROA	0.02	-0.04	0.01	-0.04	-0.04	0	-0.01	-0.01	-0.13	-0.17	0.03	0.31	-0.46	1				
TQ	0.01	-0.05	-0.03	0.07	0.08	-0.01	-0.01	-0.04	-0.1	-0.15	0.03	-0.03	-0.32	0.25	1			
P_SENSITIVE	0.02	0.17	-0.08	-0.05	-0.05	0.07	0.05	0.28	0.39	-0.02	0.03	-0.03	-0.02	-0.03	-0.12	1		
P_RESISTANT	0.01	0.1	0.15	0.14	0.12	0.05	0.02	-0.07	0.36	-0.1	0.03	-0.01	-0.12	0.11	0.16	0.07	1	
PROMOTERS	-0.01	-0.05	-0.19	-0.05	-0.03	-0.13	0	-0.1	-0.08	-0.06	0.01	0.03	-0.06	0.03	0.16	-0.34	-0.47	1

Note: The table reports the Pearson correlation coefficients for the variables used in the study. Refer to Table 1.1 for a detailed description of the variables.

members (B_FEMALE) is a mere 4.4%. Similarly, the proportion of independent female board members is only 2.6% even though the mean overall board independence (BIND) stands at 50%.

Correlation analysis was carried out to check for multicollinearity among independent variables used in the study. The results of the analysis are documented in Table 1.3. As can be seen from the table, independent variables used in the analysis are not highly correlated. As a robustness check, Variance Inflation Factor (VIF) analysis was undertaken and VIF values were within the generally acceptable limits (<5). Therefore, multicollinearity is not a concern for the analysis.

5. EMPIRICAL RESULTS

Results of the logit and tobit regression analyses are reported in Tables 1.4 and 1.5, respectively. Empirical results using both logit and tobit models are largely consistent. Both board size (BSIZE) and board independence (BIND) have a positive association with dividend payout decision. These results are consistent with other studies (e.g., see Chen et al., 2017). Similarly, audit committee independence (AIND) is also positively associated with greater dividend payouts. Overall, there is strong and consistent evidence across all eight models that the dividend payout is positively associated with board size, board independence, and audit committee independence. However, number of board meetings (BMEETINGS) is not significantly associated with dividend payouts. These results provide support to the view that directors in firms with larger boards and greater board independence may be using high dividend payouts to reduce agency problems due to free cash flows. In a similar vein, improved monitoring due to greater audit committee independence may be associated with high dividend payout decisions.

In terms of gender diversity on the board, from "Model 1" and "Model 5," we can observe that greater proportion of female directors (B_FEMALE) on the board is negatively associated with dividend payouts. "Model 2" and "Model 6" include the number of independent female directors (FEMALE_IND) along with the number of female directors on the board. Again, the results show that greater representation of "independent" female directors is negatively associated with dividend payout for the firm. Two things here are important to note that the proportion of female directors on the board is a mere 4.4%. Similarly, proportion of independent female directors is much smaller percentage at 2.6%. Frequency of board meetings (BMEETINGS) does not appear to be significantly associated with dividend payouts. As can be expected, decision to pay higher dividends is associated with greater firm profitability (ROA). In terms of ownership variables, from logit analysis, the propensity to pay dividends is negatively associated with increase in promoter shareholdings (PROMOTER) in the firm. However, propensity to pay dividends is positively associated with the increase in pressure-sensitive institutional shareholders (P_SENSITIVE). This may be because shareholders might be expecting dividend payouts to compensate for the perceived ineffective monitoring by pressure-sensitive institutional investors. Finally, propensity to pay dividends is positively associated with firm age (FAGE).

Table 1.4. Logistic Regression Analysis.

Parameter	Model 1	Model 2	Model 3	Model 4
	Estimate	Estimate	Estimate	Estimate
CONSTANT	−2.6195***	−2.7559***	−2.3733***	−2.511***
	(<0.0001)	(<0.0001)	(0.0003)	(0.0001)
BSIZE	0.0398**	0.0381**	0.0377**	0.0358**
	(0.0137)	(0.018)	(0.0205)	(0.0273)
BIND	1.546***	1.7594***	1.8422***	2.0713***
	(0.0016)	(0.0004)	(0.0002)	(<0.0001)
B_FEMALE	−4.0056***	−1.5665	−3.8659***	−1.4079
	(<0.0001)	(0.2294)	(<0.0001)	(0.2781)
FEMALE_IND		−4.1135**		−4.1935***
		(0.0102)		(0.0084)
AIND	1.58***	1.5405***	1.5446***	1.503***
	(<0.0001)	(<0.0001)	(<0.0001)	(<0.0001)
BMEETINGS	0.0608	0.0565	0.0534	0.0489
	(0.1952)	(0.227)	(0.2591)	(0.2997)
FAGE	0.0158***	0.0158***	0.0131***	0.0129***
	(<0.0001)	(<0.0001)	(<0.0001)	(<0.0001)
LOG_ASSETS	0.1388***	0.1459***	0.0989	0.1065*
	(0.0056)	(0.0037)	(0.1008)	(0.0777)
LIQUIDITY	7.9935***	8.0744***	7.8567**	7.911**
	(0.0048)	(0.0044)	(0.0055)	(0.0051)
TANGIBLE_ASSETS	0.1825	0.1871	0.1546	0.1592
	(0.6248)	(0.6151)	(0.68)	(0.6706)
RD_SALES	−1.323	−1.2446	−1.3484	−1.2605
	(0.4755)	(0.501)	(0.4604)	(0.4899)
LEVERAGE	−0.6477	−0.6859	−0.6037	−0.6444
	(0.1208)	(0.1006)	(0.152)	(0.1264)
ROA	25.1361***	25.0695***	25.0153***	24.9826***
	(<0.0001)	(<0.0001)	(<0.0001)	(<0.0001)
TQ	−0.2165***	−0.2166***	−0.1941***	−0.1941***
	(<0.0001)	(<0.0001)	(<0.0001)	(<0.0001)
PROMOTERS	−0.0124***	−0.0117***	−0.0115**	−0.0109**
	(0.0006)	(0.0013)	(0.0147)	(0.0215)
P_SENSITIVE			0.0604***	0.0608***
			(0.0009)	(0.0008)
P_RESISTANT			−0.009	−0.00929
			(0.2855)	(0.2744)
No. of observations	3,919	3,919	3,919	3,919
Chi-square (likelihood ratio)	905.0587	911.9117	921.2235	928.427
Pr > chi-square	<0.0001	<0.0001	<0.0001	<0.0001
Pseudo R-square	0.3985	0.4012	0.4048	0.4076

Note: The table reports logistic regression results using year and industry fixed effects. The table also reports the number of observations used for the analysis and Pseudo R-squared statistic. Chi-square (likelihood ratio) and Pr>chi-square statistics are also included. Refer to Table 1.1 for a detailed description of the variables. Pr>chi-square is reported in the parenthesis.

*** denotes significance at 1%, ** denotes significance at 5%, and * denotes significance at 10%.

Table 1.5. Tobit Regression Analysis.

Parameter	Model 5	Model 6	Model 7	Model 8
	Estimate	Estimate	Estimate	Estimate
CONSTANT	−0.1958	−0.2130	−0.1752	−0.1921
	(−1.59)	(−1.73)	(−1.42)	(−1.55)
BSIZE	0.0145***	0.0145***	0.0146***	0.0146***
	(4.88)	(4.89)	(4.92)	(4.93)
BIND	0.2928**	0.3221**	0.3175**	0.3453***
	(2.99)	(3.25)	(3.2)	(3.44)
B_FEMALE	−0.3727**	−0.0187	−0.3389*	0.0032
	(−1.98)	(−0.07)	(−1.79)	(0.01)
FEMALE_IND		−0.6707*		−0.6519*
		(−1.94)		(−1.89)
AIND	0.1735***	0.1670***	0.1732***	0.1668***
	(4.12)	(3.96)	(4.12)	(3.95)
BMEETINGS	0.0109	0.0107	0.0096	0.0094
	(1.17)	(1.14)	(1.03)	(1.01)
FAGE	0.0025***	0.0025***	0.0024***	0.0024***
	(5.04)	(5.01)	(4.61)	(4.58)
LOG_ASSETS	−0.0078	−0.0068	−0.0200	−0.0187
	(−0.84)	−0.72	−1.74	−1.62
LIQUIDITY	−0.0591	−0.0547	−0.0648	−0.0604
	(−0.6)	(−0.56)	(−0.66)	(−0.62)
TANGIBLE_ASSETS	−0.0784	−0.0780	−0.0685	−0.0683
	(−1.0)	(−0.99)	(−0.87)	(−0.86)
RD_SALES	−0.8623**	−0.8759**	−0.8451**	−0.8606**
	(−2.42)	(−2.42)	(−2.43)	(−2.44)
LEVERAGE	−0.3530***	−0.3634***	−0.3298***	−0.3405***
	(−4.13)	(−4.24)	(−3.83)	(−3.94)
ROA	0.7710***	0.7579***	0.7542***	0.7414***
	(4.49)	(4.42)	(4.39)	(4.32)
TQ	−0.0022	−0.0020	−0.0024	−0.0022
	(−0.42)	(−0.38)	(−0.45)	(−0.4)
PROMOTERS	−0.0007	−0.0007	0.0003	0.0003
	(−1.07)	(−1.03)	(0.29)	(0.3)
P_SENSITIVE			0.0056**	0.0054**
			(2.21)	(2.16)
P_RESISTANT			0.0014	0.0014
			(0.87)	(0.85)
Number of observations	3,919	3,919	3,919	3,919
Log likelihood	−3,961	−3,959	−3,958	−3,956
AIC	7,954	7,952	7,953	7,951

Note: The table reports tobit regression results using year and industry fixed effects. The table also reports the number of observations used for the analysis and model fit statistics (Log likelihood and AIC). Refer to Table 1.1 for a detailed description of the variables. *t*-Value is reported in the parenthesis.
*** denotes significance at 1%, ** denotes significance at 5%, and * denotes significance at 10%.

6. POLICY IMPLICATIONS AND CONCLUSIONS

The study attempts to understand the relationship between corporate governance mechanisms, board gender diversity, and ownership structure on dividend payout decisions in an emerging economy like India. Prior studies in the developed economies such as USA have found that greater representation of female members on the board is associated with higher dividend payouts. However, evidence from India shows that increase in female representation by regulation need not have the same impact on the propensity to pay dividends. The Indian Companies Act (2013) mandates an increased representation of female board members on the board. Firstly, even with regulation, the representation of the female members is woefully low at 4.4% and the proportion of independent female board members is even lower. Also, it appears that the nominal increase in female directorship appears only as a tokenism and market may not be perceiving them as "independent" players on the board. This does not however mean that the female representation on the boards should go down, on the contrary, a strong argument can be made that female director representation should go up substantially away from "tokenism" where corporate boards are traditionally dominated by their male counterparts. In this context, regulation may only be a first necessary step but not sufficient.

In terms of policy implications, prior research suggests that:

> even one woman can make a positive contribution, that having two women is generally an improvement, but that corporations with three or more women on their boards tend to benefit most from women's contributions. Three women normalizes women directors' presence, allowing women to speak and contribute more freely and men to listen with more open minds. (Konrad, Kramer, & Erkut, 2008)

Therefore, mere "tokenism" of appointing one woman board member may not be sufficient, and results from this study show "tokenism" may not work. Also, there needs to be a deliberate attempt at the board level to actively include women on the board. Board subcommittees such as nomination committee should be sensitized about these issues and if need be can formulate affirmative actions in this regard. Policy makers may want to work in this direction. Also, as it stands, the deterrence to noncompliance of these regulations seems to be minimal which allows companies to flout the prescribed norms.

In terms of other board characteristics, propensity to pay higher dividends is associated with larger boards, greater board independence and greater audit committee independence. Also, the propensity to pay dividends is higher for profitable companies. In terms of ownership structure, increase in pressure-sensitive institutional investors is associated with higher dividend payouts. This may indicate that higher dividends are a means to compensate for the limited monitoring role performed by pressure-sensitive institutional investors.

NOTES

1. http://ebook.mca.gov.in/Actpagedisplay.aspx?PAGENAME=17533
2. Provided that a company may appoint more than 15 directors after passing a special resolution.

REFERENCES

Adams, R., & Ferreira, D. (2009). Women in the boardroom and their impact on governance and performance. *Journal of Financial Economics, 94*, 291–309.

Ahern, K., & Dittmar, A. (2012). The changing of the boards: The impact on firm valuation of mandated female board representation. *The Quarterly Journal of Economics, 127*(1), 137–197.

Almazan, A., Hartzell, J. C., & Starks, L. T. (2005). Active institutional shareholders and cost of monitoring: Evidence from executive compensation. *Financial Management, 34*, 5–34.

Brickley, J., Lease, R., & Smith, C. (1988). Ownership structure and voting on Antitakeover Amendments. *Journal of Financial Economics, 20*, 267–292.

Chen, J., Leung, W. S., & Goergen, M. (2017). The impact of board gender composition on dividend payouts. *Journal of Corporate Finance, 43*, 86–105.

Cornett, M. M., Marcus, A., Saunders, A., & Tehranian, H. (2007). The impact of institutional ownership on corporate operating performance. *Journal of Banking & Finance, 31*(6), 1771–1794.

Dezso, C., & Ross, D. (2012). Does female representation in top management improve firm performance? A panel data investigation. *Strategic Management Journal, 33*, 1072–1089.

Easterbrook, F. (1984). *Two agency-cost explanations of dividends. American Economic Review, 74*, 650–659.

Faccio, M., Marchica, M. T., & Mura, R. (2016). CEO gender, corporate risk-taking, and the efficiency of capital allocation. *Journal of Corporate Finance, 39*, 193–209.

Gompers, P. A., Ishii, J. L., & Metrick, A. (2003). Corporate governance and equity prices. *The Quarterly Journal of Economics, 118*(1), 107–155.

Gul, F. A., Srinidhi, B., & Ng, A. C. (2011). Does board gender diversity improve the informativeness of stock prices? *Journal of Accounting and Economics, 51*, 314–338.

Hu, A., & Kumar, P. (2004). Managerial entrenchment and payout policy. *Journal of Financial and Quantitative Analysis, 39*, 759–790.

Jensen, M. C. (1986). Agency costs of free cash flow, corporate finance, and takeovers. *American Economic Review, 76*, 323–329.

John, K., & Senbet, L. W. (1998). Corporate governance and board effectiveness. *Journal of Banking & Finance, 22*, 371–403.

Konrad, A., Kramer, V., & Erkut, S. (2008). Critical mass: The impact of three or more women on corporate boards. *Organizational Dynamics, 37*, 145–164.

Levi, M., Li, K., & Zhang, F. (2014). Director gender and mergers and acquisitions. *Journal of Corporate Finance, 28*, 185–200.

Matsa, D. A., & Miller, A. R. (2013). *A female style in corporate leadership? Evidence from quotas. American Economic Journal: Applied Economics, 5*, 136–169.

Miller, T., & Triana, M. D. C. (2009). Demographic diversity in the boardroom: Mediators of the board diversity-firm performance relationship. *Journal of Management Studies, 46*, 755–786.

Rozeff, M. S. (1982). Growth, beta and agency costs as determinants of dividend payout ratios. *Journal of Financial Research, 3*, 249–259.

Shlifer, A., & Vishny, R. (1997). A survey of corporate governance. *Journal of Finance, 52*, 737–783.

Vinjamury, R. S. (2020). Corporate board subcommittees and firm performance: Evidence from India. *Research in Finance, 36*, 187–200.

CHAPTER 2

DO COUNTRY-LEVEL AND FIRM-LEVEL GOVERNANCE QUALITY INFLUENCE BANK SUSTAINABILITY PERFORMANCE?

Refin Dimas Pratama and Ancella Anitawati Hermawan

ABSTRACT

Governance can often be assessed as one part of directing companies' action toward something better. This study examines how governance quality at the country level and firm level can affect sustainability performance that aligns with sustainable development goals (SDG). Prior academic literature explains that if a country has a low institutional condition, it is a great challenge to implement sustainability. However, the internal awareness of the company to implement sustainability plays an important role as well. To examine the research question, this study uses the banking sector as a research sample with an observation period from 2017 to 2019. Prior literature overlooks research in the banking sector and does not feature country-level governance with firm-level governance. The data were collected either from the annual report or sustainability report, which comprises 141 companies, with the total observation of 423 firm-year. This study used panel data regression analysis and was based on the Hausman Test; it shows that random effect is used to test the hypothesis. This research finds that good quality governance at the country level, results in good sustainability performance. However, contrary to expectations regarding the quality of firm-level governance, which is thought to be positively related to sustainability performance, this study found a negative relationship.

Contemporary Issues in Financial Economics: Evidence from Emerging Economies
Research in Finance, Volume 37, 15–37
Copyright © 2023 by Emerald Publishing Limited
All rights of reproduction in any form reserved
ISSN: 0196-3821/doi:10.1108/S0196-382120230000037002

The argument that might answer the finding is the existence of governance con-ditions at the state level and at the firm level that mutually subsidize each other. This research contributes to policymakers continuing to provide counseling and improve institutional conditions to motivate companies to support the achieve-ment of the SDGs. Companies should also pay attention to the effectiveness of their internal governance and strive to use stakeholder opinions as a guide in the realization of SDGs.

Keywords: Sustainable development goals; World Governance Index; board of directors; bank; sustainability; governance

JEL Classifications: G34; M41; Q01; Q56

INTRODUCTION

The quality of environmental, social, and economic has declined in several countries, and it has become the concern of the international community such as the United Nations (UN). The emergence of the millennium development goals (MDG) in 2000 became a further initiative to solve the sustainability problem. However, MDG is still not enough to resolve the problem related to environmental problems and social problems as well (Wysokińska, 2017). Furthermore, MDG has been replaced in 2015 with SDG which has more comprehensive indicators and goals, more specifically, 17 goals and 169 indicators. Industries such as energy, manufacturing, mining, or agriculture are generally becoming a public concern due to their operational activities having a direct negative impact on the environment and communities. On the other side, the financial sector is often overlooked by a researcher, especially the banking sector. Therefore, the focus of this research is to see how the banking sector tries to actualize sustainability concepts that align with SDGs.

The sustainability topic then developed into something that not only talked about the nonfinancial sector but also emphasized the financial sector. The term sustainable finance has arisen the focus of which is related to an investment decision. According to the European Commission (2020), sustainable finance is

the process of taking due account of environmental, social, and governance considerations when making investment decisions in the financial sector, leading to increased longer-term investments into sustainable economic activities and projects.

Banking, as a sector with a more significant number of stakeholders than other sectors (Castelo, 2013), faces a lot of pressure caused some part of its activity is primarily related to investing and financing. The banking sector is considered to have a vital role in directing its clients to pay attention to sustainability aspects (Scholtens, 2009; Weber, 2018).

If a company wants to be able to do sustainability activities that align with SDGs, they need a mechanism that can configure the SDG to run well. One of the tools capable of actualizing sustainability activities that align with SDGs is governance (Van Zeijl-Rozema, Cörvers, Kemp, & Martens, 2008). Until now, governance dimensions that can boost the achievement of sustainability are still unclear. Prior literature still looked at governance as a different part, both at the country level (Kaufmann & Lafarre, 2020; Saona & San Martín, 2016) and firm level (Chams & García-Blandón, 2019; Kouaib, Mhiri, & Jarboui, 2020; Naciti, 2019), also how both of them associate with sustainability performance. This research examines both qualities of governance toward three sustainability aspects, namely economic, social, and environmental, using a banking sector in emerging markets and developed countries. This research uses an observation period between 2017 and 2019. The banking sector tends to be considered carbon-free, assuming that banking has a good reputation. However, the banking sector with its vital role in the economy (Aracil, Nájera-Sánchez, & Forcadell, 2021; Yip & Bocken, 2018) has given a negative effect through its financing activities. The banking sector should have awareness of its activities and actively participate to support SDG.

The quality of country-level governance will be measured using the World Bank index which is called the World Governance Index (WGI). While the quality of firm level will be measured using a composite score based on board characteristics such as board independence, board size, women on board, and board frequency of meetings. This research found that the quality of country level was high; it could improve companies' sustainability performance that aligns with SDGs. This result contributes to the government maintaining its institutional quality through monitoring policy implementation, law enforcement, supervision of corruption, and political stability (PS). The goal is that if the quality of country-level governance is already high, companies' motivation can also increase to support the achievement of the SDGs.

LITERATURE REVIEW AND HYPOTHESIS DEVELOPMENT

Governance can be classified into two categories (Claessens & Yurtoglu, 2013). The first category sees that governance is a set of behavioral patterns, in which these behaviors are related to performance, growth efficiency, financial structure, and treatment of shareholders and stakeholders. The second category is governance as a normative framework that regulates company operations, whether derived from the legal, judicial, or capital market systems. Meanwhile, Kaufmann, Kraay, and Mastruzzi (2011) define governance as something even broader, namely the process of government elections, the capacity of the government to implement policies, and the respect of society and the state itself for the institutions that regulate the economy and society.

On the other hand, issues related to sustainability are often associated with governance mechanisms in a company (Manning, Braam, & Reimsbach, 2019; Naciti, 2019; Zaid, Wang, Adib, Sahyouni, & Abuhijleh, 2020) or the country (Banerjee, Gupta, & McIver, 2019; Ioannou & Serafeim, 2012; Kaufmann & Lafarre, 2020).

Governance is also seen as an essential and urgently needed control tool (Glass & Newig, 2019; Van Zeijl-Rozema et al., 2008). According to Glass and Newig (2019), there is also no known dimension of governance that is most conducive to achieving sustainability. Many previous studies have explained the relationship between state-level governance and sustainability through an institutional theory approach. This theory states that every company's business activity is influenced by the regulation and presence of nongovernmental organizations that oversee company behavior (Baldini, Maso, Liberatore, Mazzi, & Terzani, 2018; Campbell, 2007; DiMaggio & Powell, 1983). The presence of the government in issuing regulations related to sustainability has an important role in motivating companies to behave ethically (Agyemang, Fantini, & Frimpong, 2015). Moreover, currently, the international community is increasingly paying attention to the issue of sustainability. Attention can be seen in the updating of the MDGs to become SDG. The SDG includes more targets and indicators than the MDGs with 17 objectives, 169 targets, and 232 indicators. The emergence of such guidelines or targets creates new pressure for companies to implement the concept of sustainability.

The implementation of sustainability in the company is also often influenced by the internal company itself. Freeman, R. E., & David, L. R. (1983) state that through the stakeholder theory approach, company knowledge related to economics, law, and philanthropy is not only aimed at shareholders but also at stakeholders. The definition of stakeholder has also been described by Freeman and David (1983). Stakeholders are groups or individuals who can influence the achievement of the company's objectives or whoever is affected by the achievement of the company's objectives. So that the company will use activities related to sustainability to establish good relations between the company and stakeholders (Michelon & Parbonetti, 2012). According to the research results of Moseñe, Burritt, Sanagustín, Moneva, and Tingey-Holyoak (2013), companies in the energy industry must be involved in social responsibility activities so that they get support from stakeholders.

In this study, governance mechanisms at the company level will focus on the role of the supervisory board or the nonexecutive board. The role of nonexecutive boards is considered to be more sensitive and responsive in responding to environmental and social issues (de Villiers, Naiker, & van Staden, 2011; Hussain, Rigoni, & Cavezzali, 2018). Chams and García-Blandón (2019) found a positive relationship between board size, gender diversity, and mean board age on sustainability. Masud, Hossain, and Kim (2018) also found that independent boards, board size, and institutional ownership have a positive influence on sustainability performance. Kouaib et al. (2020) examined the effect of the three aspects of sustainability on board effectiveness. It was found that the effectiveness of the board had a positive influence on all three aspects of sustainability.

Countrylevel Governance as a Determinant of Sustainability Performance

Several previous studies have looked at how the quality of governance at the country level can affect the sustainability performance of companies. To capture the dimensions of governance at the country level, this study will use the

WGI published by the World Bank. The WGI is composed of several dimensions, including voice and accountability (VA), PS, government effectiveness (GE), regulatory quality (RQ), rule of law (RL), and control of corruption (CC). Ojeka et al. (2019) found that when a country's institutional quality is weak, it can affect company performance. These findings are in line with Kaufmann and Lafarre (2020) who also use WGI to measure the quality of state governance and find a positive relationship with the company's sustainability performance. Rosati and Faria (2019) state that SDG in companies requires commitment from the government where the company operates. Education provided by the government regarding SDGs is very much needed because SDGs have a fairly high level of complexity. Gunawan, Permatasari, and Tilt (2020) also see that the low involvement of companies in Indonesia in supporting SDGs is due to the low understanding of Indonesian companies.

The openness of democracy that occurs in a country can support the achievement of sustainability performance. This is based on two views: First, collaboration can be created more easily between government and nongovernment (Ansell & Gash, 2008; Glass & Newig, 2019). Collaboration can generate understanding of each other and increase trust. Second, a democracy needs media. Junsheng, Akhtar, Masud, Rana, and Banna (2019) see that the role of the media can create sensitivity, increase understanding, and shape behavior to care about climate change. Countries with high VA levels are expected to affect the company's sustainability performance.

PS is also considered to be able to affect the sustainability performance of a company. The political instability of a country can interfere with the effectiveness of policy implementation (Fredriksson & Svensson, 2003). This is because the government's focus is fragmented and supervision in the implementation of policies related to sustainability will be low. So when a country has a stable political condition, according to Fredriksson, it will be far more optimal for companies to implement policies related to sustainability.

The effectiveness of the government talks about how the bureaucratic system in a country is. A bureaucratic system that is too complicated, can result in losses for other parties. Resources issued by the company only for bureaucratic purposes will interfere with the company's desire to initiate corporate social responsibility (CSR) or SDG activities (Kaufmann & Lafarre, 2020). When companies are in a country with a low level of bureaucracy, it is hoped that their initiatives to support SDG will be much easier.

The quality of the regulators in turn can also affect the company's sustainability performance. With a regulation that is enforced strictly, the level of community compliance is expected to be much higher. Strict regulations can also influence managers' behavior to be more socially responsible (Orlitzky, Louche, Gond, & Chapple, 2017). It is hypothesized that the implementation of strict regulations can improve the implementation of sustainability in the company.

RL is public awareness and trust in a rule that has been made (Kaufmann et al., 2011). Awareness of a rule can determine the success rate of implementing rules other than strict regulatory oversight. Castiglione, Infante, and Smirnova (2015) found that when a country's RL is high, the level of pollution in that country will be much lower. It is hypothesized that with a high RL in a country, the company's sustainability performance will be better.

The last one is related to controlling corruption in a country. Kaufmann et al. (2011) state that corruption control is an oversight of the abuse of power by a party to provide benefits to itself illegally. Corruption can also be reflected as negative behavior and violating the RL. When acts of corruption are not controlled in a country, ethical behavior has no value. Meanwhile, if the corruption can be controlled, the condition of the government in a country is more conducive and can provide an incentive for companies that are active in carrying out sustainable activities such as tax relief, financial assistance, or awards. It is hoped that the low level of corruption in a country can improve the company's sustainability performance.

Thus, this study will hypothesize that the high level of country-level governance quality will have a positive impact on the company's sustainability performance.

H1a. **Higher-quality country-level governance will improve the economic aspect of sustainability performance.**

H1b. **Higher-quality country-level governance will improve the social aspect of sustainability performance.**

H1c. **Higher quality of country-level governance will improve the environmental aspect of sustainability performance.**

Firm-level Governance as a Determinant of Sustainability Performance

The existence of a supervisory board in the company is considered capable of increasing company awareness to apply the concept of sustainability (Hussain, Rigoni, & Cavezzali, 2018). The company's supervisory board is required to supervise, evaluate the actions of managers, and carry out endorsements (Naciti, 2019). The supervisory board is also asked to oversee the company's strategy and objectives. The supervisory board is in a better position than the executive in protecting the interests of some shareholders and stakeholders (Cheng & Courtenay, 2006; Manning et al., 2019; Prado-Lorenzo & Garcia-Sanchez, 2010). It is hoped that companies with high-quality corporate-level governance will provide better corporate sustainability performance. In this study, the quality of corporate-level governance will be seen from the characteristics of the supervisory board, including the independent board, board size, attendance of the women's board, and the number of supervisory board meetings. In stakeholder theory, it is also said that greater diversity on a board will provide better opportunities to engage with other stakeholders, introduce social welfare objectives, commitment and concern for the environment, and an ethical approach that can complement financial goals (Hillman, Keim, & Luce, 2001).

The size of the supervisory board is one of the dimensions of governance that is often used to see the impact on sustainability performance. The larger board size will bring benefits to the company because it tends to have more diverse abilities, experiences, and resources so that it can provide good input to management (Amran, Lee, & Devi, 2014; Katmon, Mohamad, Norwani, & Farooque, 2019). However, several studies also state that the larger the board, the lower the effectiveness in decision-making. Previous research has indeed still found mixed test results between board size and sustainability performance. This study will hypothesize that a larger board size will indicate better board quality.

In stakeholder theory, independent boards tend to pay more attention to issues related to stakeholders and are not burdened with fulfilling shareholder interests (Hussain, Rigoni, & Cavezzali, 2018; Mahmood, Kouser, Ali, Ahmad, & Salman, 2018). The presence of an independent board can also encourage companies to pay attention to sustainability practices as a way of maintaining a reputation (Amran et al., 2014). Previous research related to independent boards and sustainability performance has found mixed results. Chang, Oh, Park, and Jang (2017), Hussain, Rigoni, and Cavezzali (2018), and Masud, Hossain, et al. (2018) find a positive relationship between independent boards and sustainability performance. Meanwhile, Haniffa and Cooke (2005) and Said, Zainuddin, and Haron (2009) found a negative relationship. However, this study will hypothesize a positive relationship between the independent board and the sustainability performance based on stakeholder theory.

Concern for social issues is higher in women (Naciti, 2019), making them one of the variables that become a concern among researchers, especially related to sustainability performance. Personally, women also tend to have modest, transparent, social, and environmental responsiveness to improve sustainability performance (Boulouta, 2013). It is hoped that the proportion of dominant women can improve the sustainability performance of a company. Previous research has found a positive relationship between the presence of women and sustainability performance (Chams & García-Blandón, 2019; Naciti, 2019). However, several researchers also found an insignificant relationship between the presence of women and sustainability performance (Amran et al., 2014; Katmon et al., 2019; Masud, Hossain, et al., 2018).

Previous research has found that the level of board meetings affects sustainability performance for the better (Hussain, Rigoni, & Cavezzali, 2018; Jizi, Salama, Dixon, & Stratling, 2014; Kouaib et al., 2020). This condition is based on the opinion that a high level of board meetings will pay more attention to social issues (Majumder, Akter, & Li, 2017). When boards meet intensively, communication will be more effective and explore more nonfinancial issues. The high level of board meetings can also increase oversight of management performance to act according to stakeholder expectations in addition to meeting shareholder needs. In this study, the level of board meetings is hypothesized to have a positive influence on sustainability performance.

H2a. **Higher quality firm-level governance will improve the economic aspect of sustainability performance.**

H2b. **Higher-quality firm-level governance will improve the social aspect of sustainability performance.**

H2c. **Higher quality firm-level governance will improve the environmental aspect of sustainability performance.**

How Different Is the Association Between Country-level and Firm-level Governance Quality and the Sustainability Performance in the Developed and Developing Countries?

Differences in awareness between developed countries and developing countries are considered and can influence how a company has social responsibility initiatives. Sharma (2019) has explained that increased awareness of CSR is because people in developed countries are starting to be aware of the possible dangers posed by company activities. Meanwhile, societies in developing countries have faced the difficult challenge of campaigning their CSR initiatives for broader impact (Sharma, 2019).

Research has been conducted by Al-Mamun and Seamer (2021) that compares the different levels of involvement between developed and developing countries from the perspective of the quality of institutions. RL, as one of the indicators, has shown that the quality of institutions in developing countries is lower than in developed countries. Developing countries are assessed to have a poor regulatory system, which increases the probability of individuals raising law and policy violations (Al-Mamun & Seamer, 2021). Therefore, Kostova, Roth, and Dacin (2008) argue that organizations that operate within a stable regulatory system tend to comply with environmental and social standards. This argument was supported by Mooneeapen, Abhayawansa, and Mamode Khan (2022) that said it is probably because the state is unlikely to be a key stakeholder. Boubakri, El Ghoul, Guedhami, and Wang (2020) have also done research that compares CSR between developed countries and developing countries using ASSET4 ESG from 2002 to 2015. Using 21 developing countries and 22 developed countries, the result shows that developed countries have both higher environmental and social scores than developing countries.

This research develops the following hypothesis based on the notion that companies in developed countries will have better country-level governance than developing countries and it is giving a good impact on their banking sustainability performance.

H3a. **Higher-quality country-level governance in the developed countries has a more vigorous effect on improving the economic aspect of sustainability performance than in the developing countries.**

H3b. **Higher-quality country-level governance in the developed countries has a more vigorous effect on improving the social aspect of sustainability performance than in the developing countries.**

H3c. **Higher-quality country-level governance in the developed countries has a more vigorous effect on improving the environmental aspect of sustainability performance than in the developing countries.**

Based on stakeholder theory, companies have embedded with stakeholders which are companies that must fulfill needs and benefits, both financial and nonfinancial aspects (Chams & García-Blandón, 2019; de Graaf & Stoelhorst, 2013; Freeman, 1994). Chams and García-Blandón (2019) already examined the association between governance and sustainability performance in the context of Europe and non-Europe. The results show that European countries tend to have better effective governance on sustainability performance than non-European countries. This result has conveyed the inference that boards in Europe are reflecting a tendency to focus on adjusting stakeholders' interests, while the boards in non-Europe are focusing on shareholder welfare (Chams & García-Blandón, 2019). Hence, this study hypothesizes that bank in a better environment will exhibit better sustainable performance.

H4a. **Higher-quality firm-level governance in the developed countries has a more vigorous effect on improving the economic aspect of sustainability performance than in the developing countries.**

H4b. **Higher-quality firm-level governance in the developed countries has a more vigorous effect on improving the social aspect of sustainability performance than in the developing countries.**

H4c. **Higher-quality firm-level governance in the developed countries has a more vigorous effect on improving the environmental aspect of sustainability performance than in the developing countries.**

RESEARCH METHODOLOGY

Sample and Data

This research was conducted using secondary data obtained through annual reports and company sustainability reports for 2017 until 2019. The sample comprised 423 firm-year observations from 141 companies for three years. The chosen sample period is based on the consideration that the regulation of SDG has been rolled out specifically in Europe and ASEAN. For example, European Commission imposed guidance related to initiatives in the financial field named Action Plan: Financing Sustainable Growth. Some countries in ASEAN also have published guidance on Sustainable Finance, such as Indonesia with POJK Number 51/POJK.03/2017; Malaysia with VBI Financing and Investment Impact Assessment Framework (VBIAF); Thailand with Sustainable Banking Guidelines—Responsible Lending; and Singapore with Guidelines on Responsible Financing. When selecting the sample, samples for developed countries were chosen considering the level of dependence of the state on the capital provided by the bank. Meanwhile, samples for emerging markets were chosen considering countries with five higher growth domestic product (GDP) in ASEAN.

Developed countries' categories consist of Denmark, Finland, France, Germany, Ireland, Italy, Japan, South Korea, Deutsch, Norway, and Sweden.

Emerging markets' categories consist of Indonesia, Malaysia, the Philippines, Singapore, and Thailand. The banking sector was chosen as the research sample because of its role in shaping the conditions for a country's sustainable development (Matuszak, Różańska, & Macuda, 2019). Banking is also expected to be the driving force and directing companies in other sectors to pay more attention to sustainability through loan schemes or investment activities.

The country-level data were collected from the World Bank database (WGI), while firm-level governance data was collected from companies' annual reports. Other variables related to country-level data, which include inflation and gross domestic product (GDP) per capita, were also collected from World Bank data. Some data related to the financial condition of companies, such as the size of company, market to book, and return on assets, were collected from Refinitiv Eikon.

Variables Measurement

Table 2.1 presents the proxies used to measure both the dependent variable and the independent variable. The quality of governance at the country level and the company level will be used as an independent variable. Each independent variable will be converted into a composite value. The quality of state-level governance is measured using the WGI which consists of the dimensions VA, PS, GE, RQ, RL, and CC. Meanwhile, the dependent variable in this study is the company's sustainability performance following the SDGs. Research conducted by Bali Swain and Yang-Wallentin (2020) has divided the items on the SDGs into three aspects of sustainability, namely economic, social, and environmental by being tested using exploratory factor analysis (EFA). The SDG indicators that have been classified into every aspect of sustainability will then be measured using a percentage proportion. This is because economic, social, and environmental aspects have different numbers of SDG indicators.

Research Model

This study used panel data regression analysis to prove the research hypothesis. The Hausman Test is conducted to determine the ordinary least square (OLS), fixed effect, or random effect testing that will be used in the study. If the Hausman Test results show the random effect chosen as the test model, then the Breusch and Pagan Lagrangian Test will be carried out to decide whether to use the OLS or random-effect model. The Hausman Test output shows that fixed-effect regression was used.

To test the dependent variable and independent variable, the model to be used is as follows:

$$SDGE_{i,t} = \beta_0 + \beta_1 CG\_GOV_{i,t} + \beta_2 CG\_FIRM_{i,t} + \beta_3 Control + \epsilon$$

$$SDGS_{i,t} = \beta_0 + \beta_1 CG\_GOV_{i,t} + \beta_2 CG\_FIRM_{i,t} + \beta_3 Control + \epsilon$$

$$SDGL_{i,t} = \beta_0 + \beta_1 CG\_GOV_{i,t} + \beta_2 CG\_FIRM_{i,t} + \beta_3 Control + \epsilon$$

where CG_GOV is country-level governance with six components, VA, PS, GE, RQ, RL, and CC. CG_FIRM is firm-level governance with four components, such as board size, women on board, board independence, and board meetings. The dependent variable is the SDG element with three components, SDGE for economic, SDGS for social, and SDGL for environmental. Detailed information about variables is shown in Table 2.1.

The country-level governance initially has a high level of multicollinearity between one dimension and another. To eliminate the multicollinearity, in the end, it was decided to form a composite value to measure the quality of governance at the country level which refers to the research of Manning et al. (2019). Each dimension of the WGI will be converted into a dummy in which the number is 1 if the score of each WGI dimension exceeds the median value and 0 and vice versa. Next, each number dimension is added to form a composite value. The measurement also applies to measures of governance at the company level which is composed of the independence of the supervisory board, board size,

Table 2.1. Measurement of an Independent Variable, Dependent Variable, and Control Variable.

Variable	Definition	Data Source
SDGE	SDG economy is measured based on the disclosure of banking CSR activities that are in line with the SDG referring to the paper: Bali Swain and Yang-Wallentin (2020) and Gunawan et al. (2020)	Companies' annual reports and sustainability report
SDGS	SDG social is measured based on the disclosure of banking CSR activities that are in line with the SDG referring to the paper: Bali Swain and Yang-Wallentin (2020) and Gunawan et al. (2020)	Companies' annual reports and sustainability report
SDGL	SDG environment is measured based on the disclosure of banking CSR activities that are in line with the SDG referring to the paper: Bali Swain and Yang-Wallentin (2020) and Gunawan et al. (2020)	Companies' annual reports and sustainability report
CGGOV	Countrylevel Governance Quality Index as measured by a composite score of the 6 WGI dimensions. Then it is converted into a dummy variable with a value of 1 if the dimension is more than the median value and 0 otherwise	World Bank
CGFIRM	The Quality Index of the Supervisory Board is measured by making dummy variables based on the median. The number 1 is given if it is more than the median, and 0 otherwise (Manning et al., 2019). These dimensions include the percentage of independent boards, attendance of women's councils, the size of the supervisory board, and the number of board meetings	Companies' annual report
GDP	Growth domestic product in the country	World Bank
INFL	Inflation is the inflation level in the country	World Bank
SIZE	Size is the natural logarithm of total asset	Thomson Reuters
MTB	Market to book ratio is the division of total equity divided by market capitalization	Thomson Reuters
ROA	Return on asset is a ratio that looks at the company's profitability by dividing net income by total assets	Thomson Reuters

attendance of the women's supervisory board, and the number of meetings of members of the supervisory board.

Robustness and Sensitivity Test

To convince the examination that has been done earlier between country-level and firm-level governance and sustainability performance, in this section, the measurement of firm-level will be changed. The analysis is based on the original sample of banks from 16 countries and the original model. This sensitivity test has the purpose of re-examining *H1* and *H2*.

The measurement of firm-level governance was changed as follows. Board size will be measured using research from Huse, Nielsen, and Hagen (2009) and Kiel and Nicholson (2003) who said the best composition board on average is five to nine people. Score 1 will be given to companies that have board members between five to nine persons. Then the proportion of board independence which is score 1 will be given to companies that have two of three board independence from a total supervisory board member, score 0 otherwise. Women on board need to exceed 30% of the total supervisory board; therefore, score of 1 will be given and 0 otherwise. This measurement is based on several regulations in the countries used for this research. Lastly, the frequency of board meetings will be valued at 1 if the company has a frequency of meeting more than the median and a value at 0 otherwise (Manning et al., 2019). In this regard, the sensitivity test aims to fill the gap that is still debated in the literature related to the ideal composition of a supervisory board and the connections between governance and sustainability performance in the detailed measurements. Regression in this section is conducted using a fixed-effect model based on the Hausman Test.

RESULT AND DISCUSSION

Descriptive Statistics

Table 2.2 shows the descriptive statistical results of the entire sample of banks in developed and developing countries over a three-year research period from 2017 to 2019. In Table 2.2, on average the sample has carried out sustainability activities that are in line with the SDG exceeding 75% in the economic, social, and environmental aspects. The results of these statistics show that banks in either developed or developing countries have high involvement in supporting SDGs. The quality of firm-level governance with a minimum score of 1 and a maximum score of 5 has a mean of 3.182. Meanwhile, the quality of state governance with a minimum score of 0 and a maximum score of 4 is having a mean of 2.255. This shows that the quality of firm-level governance tends to be better than country-level governance.

Table 2.3 shows the results of the correlation between variables. From this table, it can be seen that the three variables of SDG aspects are correlated with a significance level of 5%. This shows that if the quality of governance both at the state and company level can affect one aspect of sustainability, this condition

Table 2.2. Summary Descriptive Statistic.

Variable Name	Mean	Std Dev	Min	Max	N
SDGE	0.819	0.205	0	1	423
SDGS	0.758	0.237	0	1	423
SDGL	0.827	0.193	0.167	1	423
CGGOV	2.255	1.181	0	4	423
CGFIRM	3.182	2.572	0	6	423
GDP	395.42	358.39	42.367	1,174.934	423
SIZE	2.064	1.248	0.341	5.212	423
MTB	19.471	2.331	13.407	24.655	423
ROA	1.427	1.285	0	10.721	423
INFL	0.007	1.011	-0.092	0.043	423

can apply to other aspects of sustainability. This condition is also in line with Hussain, Rigoni, and Cavezzali (2018) test which sees the correlation of the sustainability index based on the global reporting initiative (GRI) as a guide for preparing sustainability reports. Then the influence of the quality of firm-level governance shows that the three aspects of sustainability have an insignificant positive result. Meanwhile, the quality of country-level governance only shows a negative relationship with SDG social aspect.

Discussion

Country-level and Firm-level Governance Quality and the Sustainability Performance
The first test carried out is related to the quality of governance on sustainability performance. The test results can be seen in Table 2.4. Multicollinearity problem is not affecting the regression result since the variance inflation factors (VIF) are below 10.

The table was tested using fixed effect regression based on the results of the Hausman Test. SDGE is an economic aspect of the company's sustainability performance. SDGS is a social aspect of the company's sustainability performance. SDGL is the environmental aspect of sustainability performance. CGGOV represents the quality of state-level governance. CGFIRM is the quality of corporate-level governance. GDP is GDP per capita in a country. SIZE is the natural logarithm of total assets. MTB is a market to book ratio calculated by dividing total equity by market capitalization. ROA is the ratio of return on assets by dividing net income by total assets. INFL is the inflation rate of a country.

Model testing shows that the fixed effect regression model was used to determine the effect of the quality of country-level governance on the sustainable performance of economic aspects. In Column 1, the results show that there is a positive influence between CGGOV and SDGE with a significance level of 5%. This positive effect remains consistent when CGGOV examines with SDGS as in Model 2. The positive effect also occurred when CGGOV was tested with SDGL as in Model 3. However, CGFIRM did not show any significant effect on either SDGE, SDGS, or SDGL. This result depicts a country with conducive governance that supports the company to have better sustainability performance.

Table 2.3. Pearson Correlation.

	SDGE	SDGS	SDGL	CGFIRM	CGGOV	GDP	INFL	SIZE	MTB	ROA
SDGE	1									
SDGS	0.8865***	1								
SDGL	0.8641***	0.7730***	1							
CGFIRM	0.0276	-0.0709	0.0136	1						
CGGOV	-0.0533	-0.1194**	-0.0249	0.5200***	1					
GDP	-0.1407***	-0.2020***	-0.0899	0.5145***	0.8919***	1				
INFL	-0.1300***	-0.0672	-0.0902	-0.4140***	-0.6257***	-0.5071***	1			
SIZE	0.4831***	0.4100***	0.3967***	0.3921***	0.4850***	0.3300***	-0.5202***	1		
MTB	-0.0192	-0.0155	-0.0337	0.1161**	0.2966***	0.2220***	-0.2399***	0.2523***	1	
ROA	0.0989**	0.0332	0.1488***	0.0498	0.0161	0.0786	-0.0202	0.1159*	-0.1832***	1

Note: Significance level: *** p-value$<1\%$, ** p-value$<5\%$, and * p-value $<10\%$.

Table 2.4. Regression Result Between Quality CG from a Country- and Firm-level Toward Sustainability Performance Align with SDG.

Variable	Expected Sign	(1) SDGE	(2) SDGS	(3) SDGL
CGGOV	+	0.038**	0.046**	0.036**
		(0.029)	(0.021)	(0.039)
CGFIRM	+	0.010	0.009	–0.009
		(0.186)	(0.264)	(0.238)
GDP	+	0.000**	0.000*	0.000
		(0.040)	(0.096)	(0.233)
INFL	–	–0.017**	–0.020*	–0.015*
		(0.034)	(0.053)	(0.096)
SIZE	+	0.084**	0.106**	0.159***
		(0.022)	(0.027)	(0.000)
MTB	–	0.003	–0.005	–0.012
		(0.376)	(0.364)	(0.173)
ROA	+	0.611	0.534	1.239*
		(0.223)	(0.306)	(0.094)
Constant		–1.032*	–1.550*	–2.424***
		(0.096)	(0.710)	(0.005)
R^2 (overall)		0.054	0.027	0.097
Prob > F		0.000	0.002	0.000
N		423	423	423

Note: The *p*-value is in brackets where *** $p<1\%$, ** $p<5\%$, and * $p <10$ (one-tailed test).

This result is also aligned with *H1a*, *H1b*, and *H1c*. This result is consistent with previous research from Rosati and Faria (2019) who argued that SDG really needed a role of state to build motivation among companies. Effective country-level governance is also assessed playing vital role in enhancing the understanding of the private sector regarding the implementation of SDG in their business environments (Betti, Consolandi, & Eccles, 2018). As a reminder, SDG constitutes an agreement among UN members that are trying to tackle the economic, social, and environmental problems that have been doubtful for everyone. Hence, the state requires to urge its individuals to implement SDG in their activities that related to them, besides the state simultaneously is giving guidance to society through policy and regulation. Banks, a highly regulated sector, are expected to fully comply with policies that are either related to climate change, economic, or social. This notion is aligned with the institutional theory that organizations are indirectly affected by regulatory institutional condition (DiMaggio & Powell, 1983; Scott, 1995).

Different results have been shown from CGFIRM and sustainability performance. The element of CGFIRM was transformed into the composite score and is found not to affect improving bank sustainability performance. Contrary to the hypothesis, this research does not prove that firm-level governance is an important variable in determining the sustainability aspect of the bank. Based on this result, it can be concluded that *H2a*, *H2b*, and *H2c* are not supported. It is indicating that the role of governance at the firm level does not have significant effect as governance at the country level.

As for control variables, the regression results show the significance for GDP and INFL (p-value < 0.05) in all three columns. The associated coefficient of GDP and INFL is shown in line as expected. Therefore, countries with favorable economic condition are more likely to enhance the bank's sustainability performance. Firm-specific control variables related to the size of the company (SIZE), market to book ratio (MTB), and return on assets (ROA), have found varying results. For instance, the size of the company is measured using a natural logarithm of total assets, showing a positive relationship and statistically significant with sustainability performance. However, MTB and ROA are not significantly correlated with sustainability performance. These results are not consistent with previous findings from prior studies which examined MTB and ROA on sustainability (Baldini et al., 2018; Naciti, 2019).

The Difference of the Association Between Country-level and Firm-level Governance Quality and the Sustainability Performance in the Developed and Developing Countries

A comparison of regression has been done to explore the different effects between developed and developing countries. Detailed information is presented in Table 2.5.

Woolridge (2013) argued that comparison regression is a tool to prove a difference between two groups through statistical examination. Table 2.5 shows that the different effects of country-level governance on the three pillars of sustainability occurred between developed and developing countries (prob $> \chi^2 < 5\%$). However, the firm-level governance shows insignificant relationship with the three pillars of sustainability. This means that the quality of firm-level governance in either developed or developing countries does not play an important role in enhancing sustainability performance in the banking sector. Based on this result, the *H3a*, *H3b*, and *H3c* are supported, while *H4a*, *H4b*, and *H4c* are not supported.

With the same purposes as the aforementioned analyses, this research also attempts to examine *H3* and *H4* by dividing the sample into subsample from developed and developing countries. Based on the Hausman Test, it shows

Table 2.5.   Regression Result to Analyze the Different Effects of Country-level and Firm-level Governance on Sustainability Performance.

Variable	SDGE	SDGS	SDGL
Prob$>\chi^2$			
CGGOV	0.029**	0.002***	0.000***
CGFIRM	0.106	0.131	0.220

Significance level: ***1%, **5%, and *10%.

that the fixed-effects model was chosen for developed countries' sample. Alternatively, the regression was performed using a random-effects model for developing countries' sample. The results reveal in Table 2.6 that developed countries show higher coefficients and significance levels than developing countries in terms of quality country-level governance. Accordingly, the results are likely aligned and robust because it shows a consistency with the results before. Moreover, the results are also consistent with the main analyses which show positive significance relationship between country-level governance and SDGE, SDGS, and SDGL. However, the firm-level governance still does not show significance relationship with sustainability performance. These results suggest that countries in developed countries have a better quality of VA, PS, GE, RQ, RL, and CC. Meanwhile, the quality of firm-level governance is homogeneous to each pillar of sustainability in the banking sector, even in developed countries. The behavior of managers regarding sustainability is directly monitored by country-level governance. This concludes that the role of the supervisory board on sustainability performance is not applicable in developed countries as well.

The results of control variables are also consistent with the main analysis, which shows that the size of company (SIZE) has a positive significance relationship with sustainability performance in both developed and developing countries. However, control variable related to GDP per capita shows the opposite result that does not align as expected. GDP per capita has a negative effect on sustainability performance in developing countries' sample. This result indicates that when GDP per capita is low, it cannot hamper the banking industry from achieving sustainability performance as long as they have a conducive quality of country-level governance (Banerjee et al., 2019).

Robustness and Sensitivity Test

The first robustness test was carried out by changing the measurement of firm-level governance (CGFIRM) and then tested using Model 1. Based on the Hausman Test, the test was carried out using the fixed-effects model. In Table 2.7, the variable quality of governance at the country-level governance (CGGOV) has a significant positive effect on the sustainability performance of economic (SDGE), social (SDGS), and environmental (SDGL) aspects. Each has a significance level below 5% (p-value $< 5\%$). Meanwhile, the regression results for robustness testing show that the variable quality of firm-level governance (IDXFIRM) still shows insignificant results. Based on these results, it can be concluded that although using different measurements, the role of governance at the country level is the most important determinant in efforts to improve the company's sustainability performance. This is because the quality of state-level governance (IDXGOV) consistently shows a significant positive effect on the three sustainability performances.

Table 2.6. Regression Result for Subsample Developed and Developing Countries.

Variable	Expected Sign	(1) SDGE	(2) SDGS	(3) SDGL
Panel A: Regression Result for Developed Countries				
CGGOV	+	0.081***	0.086**	0.059**
		(0.005)	(0.016)	(0.039)
CGFIRM	+	−0.006	0.006	−0.019
		(0.378)	(0.411)	(0.185)
GDP	+	0.000	0.000	0.000
		(0.120)	(0.243)	(0.351)
INFL	−	−0.034*	−0.038	−0.036*
		(0.082)	(0.113)	(0.084)
SIZE	+	0.253***	0.345***	0.401***
		(0.004)	(0.003)	(0.000)
MTB	−	0.003	−0.005	−0.010
		(0.397)	(0.370)	(0.216)
ROA	+	0.711	−0.346	0.038
		(0.365)	(0.449)	(0.494)
Constant		−4.766**	−6.715***	−7.552***
		(0.006)	(0.003)	(0.000)
R^2 (Overall)		0.164	0.223	0.178
Prob > F		0.001	0.005	0.000
N		207	2017	207
Panel B: Regression Result for Developing Countries				
IDXGOV	+	0.025*	0.040**	0.045***
		(0.068)	(0.018)	(0.005)
IDXFIRM	+	−0.012	−0.018	−0.019*
		(0.145)	(0.107)	(0.074)
GDP	+	−0.000**	−0.000**	−0.000***
		(0.015)	(0.042)	(0.004)
INFL	−	−0.017**	−0.016*	−0.012
		(0.019)	(0.067)	(0.119)
SIZE	+	0.058***	0.058***	0.052***
		(0.000)	(0.000)	(0.000)
MTB	−	0.018	0.013	0.024*
		(0.142)	(0.255)	(0.092)
ROA	+	0.694	0.305	1.392*
		(0.166)	(0.371)	(0.053)
Constant		−0.258*	−0.343**	−0.225
		(0.065)	(0.041)	(0.108)
R^2 (Overall)		0.435	0.347	0.354
Prob > F		0.000	0.000	0.000

SDGE is an economic aspect of the company's sustainability performance. SDGS is a social aspect of the company's sustainability performance. SDGL is the environmental aspect of sustainability performance. CGGOV represents the quality of state-level governance. CGFIRM is the quality of corporate-level governance. GDP is GDP per capita in a country. SIZE is the natural logarithm of total assets. MTB is a market to book ratio calculated by dividing total equity by market capitalization. ROA is the ratio of return on assets by dividing net income by total assets. INFL is the inflation rate of a country. The p-value is in brackets where *** $p<1\%$, ** $p<5\%$, and * $p<10\%$ (one-tailed test).

Table 2.7. Sensitivity Analyses Test.

Variable	Expected Sign	(1) SDGE	(2) SDGS	(3) SDGL
CGGOV	+	0.035**	0.048**	0.038**
		(0.020)	(0.017)	(0.028)
CGFIRM	+	−0.012	−0.001	−0.016
		(0.154)	(0.470)	(0.113)
GDP	+	0.000**	0.000*	0.000
		(0.035)	(0.093)	(0.212)
INFL	−	−0.018**	−0.021**	−0.016*
		(0.026)	(0.048)	(0.078)
SIZE	+	0.082**	0.104**	0.157***
		(0.025)	(0.029)	(0.001)
MTB	−	0.004	−0.004	−0.011
		(0.340)	(0.382)	(0.196)
ROA	+	0.692	0.566	1.340*
		(0.194)	(0.296)	(0.078)
Constant		−0.964	−1.488*	−2.359***
		(0.112)	(0.078)	(0.006)
R^2 (Overall)		0.095	0.078	0.096
N		423	423	423

SDGE is an economic aspect of the company's sustainability performance. SDGS is a social aspect of the company's sustainability performance. SDGL is the environmental aspect of sustainability performance. CGGOV represents the quality of state-level governance. CGFIRM is the quality of corporate-level governance. GDP is GDP per capita in a country. SIZE is the natural logarithm of total assets. MTB is a market to book ratio calculated by dividing total equity by market capitalization. ROA is the ratio of return on assets by dividing net income by total assets. INFL is the inflation rate of a country.

The *p*-value is in brackets where *** $p<1\%$, ** $p<5\%$, and * $p<10\%$ (one–tailed test).

CONCLUSION

In this study, questions related to the determinants of sustainability performance have been tested using the quality of governance at the state and company levels. Different from previous studies that looked at governance partially, in this study both governances were tested simultaneously concerning three sustainability aspects. Previous research has also looked at sustainability performance based on the GRI framework or the environmental, social, and governance score (Baldini et al., 2018), while this research refers to the objectives of the SDGs.

Based on the results of the analysis that has been carried out on the quality of governance and sustainability performance, some interesting results are found. The quality of governance at the country level has a positive influence on all aspects of sustainability, even when tested partially. However, contrary to expectations regarding the quality of corporate-level governance which is thought to be positively related to sustainability performance, this study found a negative relationship. The argument that might answer the finding is the existence of governance conditions at the state level and at the company level, which mutually subsidizes each other. This negative relationship also proves the opinion of Agyemang et al. (2015) and Campbell (2007) who emphasize the importance of the presence of government to motivate companies to care for their communities. Even so, different governance characteristics remain an important part of improving the company's social and environmental performance (Hussain, Rigoni, & Cavezzali, 2018). Hence even when the corporate level governance dimension is low, they are still able to produce better sustainability performance. This study also shows that the effect of a country's GDP condition does not prevent companies from being involved in supporting SDGs. This is in line with the findings of Banerjee et al. (2019) who found that GDP was negatively related to corporate sustainability practices.

Research is limited in the process of testing governance variables and sustainability performance. First, the process of measuring sustainability performance that is in line with the SDGs does not consider the frequency of company initiatives for each SDG objective. Second, the interpretation of the relationship between corporate-level governance and sustainability performance is not analyzed in every dimension of sustainability. It is hoped that further research can show how each dimension of sustainability can relate to aspects of sustainability. Third, the process of measuring the sustainability performance according to the SDGs is only done alone without any validity and reliability tests. There are several avenues for future research to address those limitations of this study. First, future studies should examine country-level governance with the other measures. Because previous literature has already examined using the WGI indicator and the need to explore another measurement to generate more robust result. Future studies could also do a research regarding to how banking sector is taking investment decision for unfriendly industry toward environment more deeply.

This research contributes to policymakers to enhance counseling and create conducive institutional conditions. It could motivate companies to support the achievement of SDGs. Companies also need to pay attention to the effectiveness of their internal governance and strive to use stakeholder opinions as a guide in the realization of SDGs.

REFERENCES

Agyemang, O. S., Fantini, G., & Frimpong, J. (2015). Does country-level governance enhance ethical behaviour of firms? An African perspective. *International Journal of Law and Management*, *57*(6), 582–599. https://doi.org/10.1108/IJLMA-12-2014-0063

Al-Mamun, A., & Seamer, M. (2021). The influence of institutional qualities on CSR engagement: A comparison of developed and developing economies. *Meditari Accountancy Research*, 30(1), 94–120. https://doi.org/10.1108/MEDAR-02-2020-0768

Amran, A., Lee, S. P., & Devi, S. S. (2014). The influence of governance structure and strategic corporate social responsibility toward sustainability reporting quality. *Business Strategy and the Environment*, *23*(4), 217–235. https://doi.org/10.1002/bse.1767

Ansell, C., & Gash, A. (2008). Collaborative governance in theory and practice. *Journal of Public Administration Research and Theory*, *18*(4), 543–571. https://doi.org/10.1093/jopart/mum032

Aracil, E., Nájera-Sánchez, J.-J., & Forcadell, F. J. (2021). Sustainable banking: A literature review and integrative framework. *Finance Research Letters*, *42*, 101932. https://doi.org/10.1016/j.frl.2021.101932

Baldini, M., Maso, L. D., Liberatore, G., Mazzi, F., & Terzani, S. (2018). Role of country- and firm-level determinants in environmental, social, and governance disclosure. *Journal of Business Ethics*, *150*(1), 79–98. https://doi.org/10.1007/s10551-016-3139-1

Bali Swain, R., & Yang-Wallentin, F. (2020). Achieving sustainable development goals: Predicaments and strategies. *International Journal of Sustainable Development and World Ecology, 27*(2), 96–106. https://doi.org/10.1080/13504509.2019.1692316

Banerjee, R., Gupta, K., & McIver, R. (2019). What matters most to firm-level environmentally sustainable practices: Firm–specific or country–level factors? *Journal of Cleaner Production, 218*, 225–240. https://doi.org/10.1016/j.jclepro.2019.02.008

Betti, G., Consolandi, C., & Eccles, R. (2018). The relationship between investor materiality and the sustainable development goals: A methodological framework. *Sustainability, 10*(7), 2248. https://doi.org/10.3390/su10072248

Boubakri, N., El Ghoul, S., Guedhami, O., & Wang, H. (2020). Corporate social responsibility in emerging market economies: Determinants, consequences, and future research directions. *Emerging Markets Review*, (June), 100758. https://doi.org/10.1016/j.ememar.2020.100758

Boulouta, I. (2013). Hidden connections: The link between board gender diversity and corporate social performance. *Journal of Business Ethics, 113*, 185–197. https://doi.org/10.1007/s10551-012-1293-7

Campbell, J. L. (2007). Why would corporations behave in socially responsible ways? an institutional theory of corporate social responsibility. *Academy of Management Review, 32*(3), 946–967. https://doi.org/10.5465/amr.2007.25275684

Castelo, B. M. (2013). *Encyclopedia of corporate social responsibility*. Heidelberg: Springer. https://doi.org/10.1007/978-3-642-28036-8

Castiglione, C., Infante, D., & Smirnova, J. (2015). Environment and economic growth: Is the rule of law the go-between? The case of high-income countries. *Energy, Sustainability and Society, 5*(1), 26. https://doi.org/10.1186/s13705-015-0054-8

Chams, N., & García-Blandón, J. (2019). Sustainable or not sustainable? The role of the board of directors. *Journal of Cleaner Production, 226*, 1067–1081. https://doi.org/10.1016/j.jclepro.2019.04.118

Chang, Y. K., Oh, W. Y., Park, J. H., & Jang, M. G. (2017). Exploring the relationship between board characteristics and CSR: Empirical evidence from Korea. *Journal of Business Ethics, 140*(2), 225–242. https://doi.org/10.1007/s10551-015-2651-z

Cheng, E. C. M., & Courtenay, S. M. (2006). Board composition, regulatory regime and voluntary disclosure. *The International Journal of Accounting, 41*(3), 262–289. https://doi.org/10.1016/j.intacc.2006.07.001

Claessens, S., & Yurtoglu, B. B. (2013). Corporate governance in emerging markets: A survey. *Emerging Markets Review, 15*, 1–33. https://doi.org/10.1016/j.ememar.2012.03.002

de Graaf, F. J., & Stoelhorst, J. W. (2013). The role of governance in Corporate Social Responsibility. *Business & Society, 52*(2), 282–317. https://doi.org/10.1177/0007650309336451

de Villiers, C., Naiker, V., & van Staden, C. J. (2011). The effect of board characteristics on firm environmental performance. *Journal of Management, 37*(6), 1636–1663. https://doi.org/10.1177/0149206311411506

DiMaggio, P. J., & Powell, W. W. (1983). The iron cage revisited: Institutional isomorphism in organizational fields. *American Sociological Review, 48*(2), 147–160. Retrieved from http://www.jstor.org/stable/2095101.

European Commission. (2020). Overview sustainable finance. Retrieved from https://ec.europa.eu/info/business-economy-euro/banking-and-finance/sustainable-finance_en. Accessed on February 25, 2021.

Fredriksson, P. G., & Svensson, J. (2003). Political instability, corruption and policy formation: The case of environmental policy. *Journal of Public Economics, 87*(7–8), 1383–1405. https://doi.org/10.1016/S0047-2727(02)00036-1

Freeman, R. E. (1994). The politics of stakeholder theory: Some future directions. *Business Ethics Quarterly, 4*(4), 409–421. https://doi.org/10.2307/3857340

Freeman, R. E., & David, L. R. (1983). Stockholders and stakeholders: A new perspective on corporate governance. *California Management Review, 25*(3), 88–106. https://doi.org/10.2307/41165018

Glass, L.-M., & Newig, J. (2019). Governance for achieving the sustainable development goals: How important are participation, policy coherence, reflexivity, adaptation and democratic institutions? *Earth System Governance, 2*, 100031. https://doi.org/10.1016/j.esg.2019.100031

Gunawan, J., Permatasari, P., & Tilt, C. (2020). Sustainable development goal disclosures: Do they support responsible consumption and production? *Journal of Cleaner Production*, *246*, 118989. https://doi.org/10.1016/j.jclepro.2019.118989

Haniffa, R. M., & Cooke, T. E. (2005). The impact of culture and governance on corporate social reporting. *Journal of Accounting and Public Policy*, *24*(5), 391–430. https://doi.org/10.1016/j.jaccpubpol.2005.06.001

Hillman, A. J., Keim, G. D., & Luce, R. A. (2001). Board composition and stakeholder performance: Do stakeholder directors make a difference? *Business & Society*, *40*(3), 295–314. https://doi.org/10.1177/000765030104000304

Huse, M., Nielsen, S. T., & Hagen, I. M. (2009). Women and employee-elected board members, and their contributions to board control tasks. *Journal of Business Ethics*, *89*(4), 581–597. https://doi.org/10.1007/s10551-008-0018-4

Hussain, N., Rigoni, U., & Cavezzali, E. (2018). Does it pay to be sustainable? Looking inside the black box of the relationship between sustainability performance and financial performance. *Corporate Social Responsibility and Environmental Management*, *25*(6), 1198–1211. https://doi.org/10.1002/csr.1631

Ioannou, I., & Serafeim, G. (2012). What drives corporate social performance the role of nation-level institutions. *Journal of International Business Studies*, *43*(9), 834–864. https://doi.org/10.1057/jibs.2012.26

Jizi, M. I., Salama, A., Dixon, R., & Stratling, R. (2014). Corporate governance and corporate social responsibility disclosure: Evidence from the US Banking Sector. *Journal of Business Ethics*, *125*(4), 601–615. https://doi.org/10.1007/s10551-013-1929-2

Junsheng, H., Akhtar, R., Masud, M. M., Rana, M. S., & Banna, H. (2019). The role of mass media in communicating climate science: An empirical evidence. *Journal of Cleaner Production*, *238*, 117934. https://doi.org/10.1016/j.jclepro.2019.117934

Katmon, N., Mohamad, Z. Z., Norwani, N. M., & Farooque, O. Al. (2019). Comprehensive board diversity and quality of corporate social responsibility disclosure: Evidence from an emerging market. *Journal of Business Ethics*, *157*(2), 447–481. https://doi.org/10.1007/s10551-017-3672-6

Kaufmann, D., Kraay, A., & Mastruzzi, M. (2011). The worldwide governance indicators: Methodology and analytical issues. *Hague Journal on the Rule of Law*, *3*(2), 220–246. https://doi.org/10.1017/S1876404511200046

Kaufmann, W., & Lafarre, A. (2020). Does good governance mean better corporate social performance? A comparative study of OECD countries. *International Public Management Journal*, *24*(6), 762–791. https://doi.org/10.1080/10967494.2020.1814916

Kiel, G. C., & Nicholson, G. J. (2003). Board composition and corporate performance: How the Australian experience informs contrasting theories of corporate governance. *Corporate Governance*, *11*(3), 189–205. https://doi.org/10.1111/1467-8683.00318

Kostova, T., Roth, K., & Dacin, M. T. (2008). Institutional theory in the study of multinational corporations: A critique and new directions. *Academy of Management Review*, *33*(4), 994–1006. https://doi.org/10.5465/amr.2008.34422026

Kouaib, A., Mhiri, S., & Jarboui, A. (2020). Board of directors' effectiveness and sustainable performance: The triple bottom line. *Journal of High Technology Management Research*, *31*(2), 100390. https://doi.org/10.1016/j.hitech.2020.100390

Mahmood, Z., Kouser, R., Ali, W., Ahmad, Z., & Salman, T. (2018). Does corporate governance affect sustainability disclosure? A mixed methods study. *Sustainability (Switzerland)*, *10*(1), 1–20. https://doi.org/10.3390/su10010207

Majumder, M. T. H., Akter, A., & Li, X. (2017). Corporate governance and corporate social disclosures: A meta-analytical review. *International Journal of Accounting and Information Management*, *25*(4), 434–458. https://doi.org/10.1108/IJAIM-01-2017-0005

Manning, B., Braam, G., & Reimsbach, D. (2019). Corporate governance and sustainable business conduct—Effects of board monitoring effectiveness and stakeholder engagement on corporate sustainability performance and disclosure choices. *Corporate Social Responsibility and Environmental Management*, *26*(2), 351–366. https://doi.org/10.1002/csr.1687

Masud, M. A. K., Hossain, M. S., & Kim, J. D. (2018). Is green regulation effective or a failure: Comparative analysis between Bangladesh Bank (BB) green guidelines and global reporting initiative guidelines. *Sustainability (Switzerland)*, *10*(4), 1267. https://doi.org/10.3390/su10041267

Matuszak, Ł., Różańska, E., & Macuda, M. (2019). The impact of corporate governance characteristics on banks' corporate social responsibility disclosure: Evidence from Poland. *Journal of Accounting in Emerging Economies*, *9*(1), 75–102. https://doi.org/10.1108/JAEE-04-2017-0040

Michelon, G., & Parbonetti, A. (2012). The effect of corporate governance on sustainability disclosure. *Journal of Management and Governance*, *16*(3), 477–509. https://doi.org/10.1007/s10997-010-9160-3

Mooneeapen, O., Abhayawansa, S., & Mamode Khan, N. (2022). The influence of the country governance environment on corporate environmental, social and governance (ESG) performance. *Sustainability Accounting, Management and Policy Journal*, *13*(4), 953–985. https://doi.org/10.1108/SAMPJ-07-2021-0298

Moseñe, J. A., Burritt, R. L., Sanagustín, M. V., Moneva, J. M., & Tingey-Holyoak, J. (2013). Environmental reporting in the Spanish wind energy sector: An institutional view. *Journal of Cleaner Production*, *40*, 199–211. https://doi.org/10.1016/j.jclepro.2012.08.023

Naciti, V. (2019). Corporate governance and board of directors: The effect of a board composition on firm sustainability performance. *Journal of Cleaner Production*, *237*, 117727. https://doi.org/10.1016/j.jclepro.2019.117727

Ojeka, S., Adegboye, A., Adegboye, K., Umukoro, O., Dahunsi, O., & Ozordi, E. (2019). Corruption perception, institutional quality and performance of listed companies in Nigeria. *Heliyon*, *5*(10), e02569. https://doi.org/10.1016/j.heliyon.2019.e02569

Orlitzky, M., Louche, C., Gond, J. P., & Chapple, W. (2017). Unpacking the drivers of corporate social performance: A multilevel, multistakeholder, and multimethod analysis. *Journal of Business Ethics*, *144*(1), 21–40. https://doi.org/10.1007/s10551-015-2822-y

Prado-Lorenzo, J. M., & Garcia-Sanchez, I. M. (2010). The role of the board of directors in disseminating relevant information on greenhouse gases. *Journal of Business Ethics*, *97*(3), 391–424. https://doi.org/10.1007/s10551-010-0515-0

Rosati, F., & Faria, L. G. D. (2019). Addressing the SDGs in sustainability reports: The relationship with institutional factors. *Journal of Cleaner Production*, *215*, 1312–1326. https://doi.org/10.1016/j.jclepro.2018.12.107

Said, R., Zainuddin, Y., & Haron, H. (2009). The relationship between corporate social responsibility disclosure and corporate governance characteristics in Malaysian public listed companies. *Social Responsibility Journal*, *5*(2), 212–226. https://doi.org/10.1108/17471110910964496

Saona, P., & San Martín, P. (2016). Country level governance variables and ownership concentration as determinants of firm value in Latin America. *International Review of Law and Economics*, *47*, 84–95. https://doi.org/10.1016/j.irle.2016.06.004

Scholtens, B. (2009). Corporate social responsibility in the international banking industry. *Journal of Business Ethics*, *86*(2), 159–175. https://doi.org/10.1007/s10551-008-9841-x

Scott, W. R. (1995). *Institutions and organizations*. California, CA: Sage.

Sharma, E. (2019). A review of corporate social responsibility in developed and developing nations. *Corporate Social Responsibility and Environmental Management*, *26*(4), 712–720. https://doi.org/10.1002/csr.1739

Van Zeijl-Rozema, A., Cörvers, R., Kemp, R., & Martens, P. (2008). Governance for sustainable development: A framework. *Sustainable Development*, *16*(6), 410–421. https://doi.org/10.1002/sd.367

Weber, O. (2018). *The financial sector and the SDGs interconnections and future directions*. CIGI Papers 201. Centre for International Governance Innovation (pp. 1–32).

Woolridge, J. (2013). *Introductory econometrics: A modern approach* (5th ed.). Mason, OH: South-Western https://doi.org/10.4324/9780203157688

Wysokińska, Z. (2017). Millennium development goals/UN and sustainable development goals/UN as instruments for realising sustainable development concept in the global economy. *Comparative Economic Research*, *20*(1), 101–118. https://doi.org/10.1515/cer-2017-0006

Yip, A. W. H., & Bocken, N. M. P. (2018). Sustainable business model archetypes for the banking industry. *Journal of Cleaner Production*, *174*, 150–169. https://doi.org/10.1016/j.jclepro.2017.10.190

Zaid, M. A. A., Wang, M., Adib, M., Sahyouni, A., & Abuhijleh, S. T. F. (2020). Boardroom nationality and gender diversity: Implications for corporate sustainability performance. *Journal of Cleaner Production*, *251*, 119652. https://doi.org/10.1016/j.jclepro.2019.119652

CHAPTER 3

EXPLORING A STATE-OWNED BANK'S ADOPTION OF SUSTAINABLE FINANCE: EVIDENCE FROM A DEVELOPING COUNTRY

Naufal Daffaveda Adam and Desi Adhariani

ABSTRACT

This study explores the implementation of sustainable finance in an Indonesian state-owned bank ("ABC Bank" or "ABC"). A case study approach is employed to deeply analyze the implementation using data collected through interviews and through a review of company documents. The frameworks from Soppe (2004) and Indonesia Regulation POJK 51 were used to examine the sustainable finance implementation. The findings show that ABC Bank exercises a sustainability commitment in implementing sustainable finance long before the government regulation is imposed on several banks as early adopters in Indonesia. The regulation requires selected banks to apply the eight principles of sustainable finance and prepare a sustainable financial action plan and sustainability report. ABC's commitment is mainly driven by its status as a government-owned bank, thus facilitating the awareness of achieving public welfare while maintaining profitability. Social implication of this study is that developing countries often face more severe consequences of climate change than developed countries. Hence, the sustainable finance implementation can have a significant social impact to reduce

Contemporary Issues in Financial Economics: Evidence from Emerging Economies
Research in Finance, Volume 37, 39–62
Copyright © 2023 by Emerald Publishing Limited
All rights of reproduction in any form reserved
ISSN: 0196-3821/doi:10.1108/S0196-382120230000037003

the negative effect. This study contributes to the literature by exploring the initial adoption of sustainable finance by a state-owned bank attempting to balance the interests of the public and management. It also provides insights into other financial institutions adopting sustainable finance as mandated by the local obligation POJK 51.

Keywords: Sustainable finance; sustainable development; state-owned bank; ethical framework; POJK 51; Indonesia

1. INTRODUCTION

With increase in awareness about the environmental impacts of economic activities, sustainable finance has become an important concept. This concept incorporates sustainability, which integrates financial, social, and environmental elements to connect the interests of present and future generations (Soppe, 2004). Several international institutions, such as the United Nations and International Finance Corporation, encourage countries to introduce and implement sustainable finance. The financing model is expected to be communicated with the central bank and commercial banks because the latter also offer loans directly to investors planning to build and do business in certain areas, which creates a direct channel to implement sustainable lending practices. Among the countries affected by the issue, Indonesia has yet to adopt and implement this financial model because it is considered to be aligned with the country's commitment to handle several sustainability issues, including reducing carbon emissions by 29% by 2030 (Goldenberg, 2015). The implementation of sustainable finance is also expected to mobilize sustainable development to meet society's current and long-term needs.

In the academic field, the rising awareness of sustainable finance has been focused predominantly on developed countries, leaving practices in developing countries, including Indonesia, largely understudied. However, it is often the developing countries that face more severe consequences of climate change. Among the thin literature, it is worth mentioning Forcadell and Aracil (2017), who found a positive impact of sustainable banking in Latin America to improve educational levels and financial inclusion, leading to poverty alleviation. As for the instrument, Banga (2019) suggested the use of a green bond market as a potential source of climate finance for developing countries. This study tried to fill the research gap regarding the lack of knowledge on how sustainable finance is implemented in developing countries.

The study of sustainable finance in the Indonesian context is important to explore the diffusion of the concept in a developing country facing several sustainability issues associated with high population density and rapid industrialization, accompanied by high poverty levels and under-resourced governance. The discussion is also relevant because the issue gained momentum after the government agency (Indonesia Authority of Financial Services – Otoritas Jasa Keuangan or OJK in brief) released a new regulation on sustainable finance called **POJK** (OJK Regulation) No. 51/POJK.03/2017. It requires the implementation of sustainable finance by financial service institutions, stock issuers, and public companies. Following this regulation, eight national banks in Indonesia, with accumulative assets of up to 46% of the country's total banking assets, together with the World Wildlife Fund (WWF), Indonesia, launched the Indonesia Sustainable Finance Initiative in mid-2018. The commitment of those banks to consider environmental practices when making lending decisions (e.g., in the controversial palm oil sector) is important to protect the environment and sets a good example for banks that have not joined the initiative. Amid this regulation's preparation turmoil by Indonesian companies, ABC Bank, which is one of the pioneers of implementation, serves as a good benchmark for other institutions in implementing the policy.

By adopting a case study approach, this study aims to answer two research questions: Have sustainable finance practices implemented by ABC Bank been consistent with the concept and framework of sustainable corporate finance? What are the challenges faced by ABC Bank in implementing sustainable finance?

ABC as the site ontology is one of the largest state-owned enterprises (SOEs) in the banking industry and is spread throughout Indonesia. ABC is listed on the Indonesia Stock Exchange and has 40% public ownership. The findings show that ABC's commitment to contribute to sustainable development has not been seen as problematic as it has implemented sustainable finance voluntarily before formal regulation is mandated. At the operational level, there are challenges in balancing the goals of public welfare and profitability as economic motives.

This study provides theoretical contributions in enriching the literature on the role of a state-owned bank with two missions – supporting public welfare and achieving company profits in internalizing the sustainable finance principle. This study attempts to contribute by portraying the practice using a framework consisting of several parameters to explore the implementation of sustainable finance in one of the first movers in Indonesia. Apart from the theoretical contributions, this study also offers a practical contribution for Indonesian organizations seeking to embrace sustainable finance by presenting an analysis of a sustainable finance implementation pilot project focusing on one state-owned bank as a case study. This study also serves as an input to regulators, especially OJK, on the analysis of implementation challenges of sustainable finance faced by a state-owned bank.

2. SUSTAINABLE FINANCE: SOME RATIONALES

Financial institutions have an important role in the economy, society, and sustainable development that makes them the component of business case for sustainability (Schaltegger, Hörisch, & Freeman, 2017). Through the implementation of sustainable finance, companies are expected to continue to grow while minimizing the negative impact on society or the environment. This has been overlooked by traditional, previous financial concepts that recommended financial profit as a company's sole purpose. Financial literature in the twentieth century was also very limited to research on the equilibrium between risk and profit (e.g., asset valuation through CAPM and APT) (Soppe, 2004). This was also used as a justification by the company seeking the highest profit without paying attention to other aspects such as social and environmental.

2.1. State-owned Bank and Sustainable Finance

Rising concerns over the environment and sustainable development pose both risks and opportunities for banks (Jeucken, 2010). The intermediary role of banks in society is significant to achieve sustainable development, as banks transform money into place, term, size, and risk in an economy that affects economic development. Financing policies and credit applications can create opportunities for a sustainable business, such as in the form of green funds for environment-friendly investments that satisfy the return or risk management requirements from a sustainability perspective (Jeucken, 2010).

Governments also have increasing concerns about the intermediary role that banks play, particularly in the achievement of environmental policies (Jeucken & Bouma, 2017). The government's awareness is translated into policy in various organizations, including SOEs as government agents, to advance change in society. Hence, the use of a state-owned bank as a case study in this research might serve as an appropriate choice to illustrate the tensions that banks face in reconciling socio-environmental objectives with the drive for profits. This is not to say that private banks are not important vehicles for channeling private savings into industrial development; however, especially in developing countries, economic institutions are not sufficiently developed to play this critical role (Srinivas & Sitorus, 2004). In this situation, governments could step in, set up financial institutions, and leverage economic and sustainable development through them.

2.2. Indonesia Regulation POJK 51 and Sustainable Finance

The role of the government in sustainable development is reflected in regulations to enhance awareness, including in specific areas such as sustainable finance adopted in the banking sector. In Indonesia, several relevant regulations have been issued; for instance, Bank Indonesia Regulation No. 14/15/PBI/2012 requires the consideration of environmental management by debtors in the credit approval process. Several activities have been conducted, such as training to evaluate credit distributions through environmental impact assessments (AMDAL – Analisis Mengenai Dampak Lingkungan). The recent POJK 51 regulation has also been enacted to support sustainable finance as an intermediary for broader social and environmental agendas: preventing environmental damage, reducing social inequality, maintaining biodiversity, and encouraging the efficient use of energy and natural resources.

The development of POJK 51 began with the issuance of a sustainable finance roadmap in Indonesia by the Financial Services Authority (OJK) in December 2014 to encourage the understanding and application of the concept of sustainable finance in Indonesia. The guide is aimed at creating a competitive but pro-growth, pro-job, pro-poor, and pro-environment business climate. The sustainable finance roadmap is published as a strategic and systematic approach to the application of the concept of sustainable finance in Indonesia by encouraging the financial services sector to play an active role in achieving the national long- and medium-term development plans.

In 2017, the OJK issued Financial Services Authority Regulation Number 51/POJK.03/2017 concerning the implementation of sustainable finance at financial service institutions, issuers, and public companies. This regulation is a follow-up to the OJK to provide technical guidance to ensure the success of the previously prepared roadmap. To prepare this POJK, the OJK requires every financial service institution, issuer, and public company to implement sustainable financial concepts in its business activities. The POJK requires three things: fulfillment of eight financial principles, preparation of the sustainable finance action plan, and preparation of sustainability reports. To apply the concept of sustainable finance and the disclosure of the two documents (sustainable finance action plan and sustainability report), POJK 51 provides different deadlines for each financial service institution as per its category. Several categories of financial service institutions exist, each with different delivery deadlines – developed by OJK to accommodate the differences in the ability and readiness of financial service institutions in Indonesia. For example, commercial banks (BUKU) 3, BUKU 4, and foreign banks are required to submit sustainability reports and a design for their first sustainable financial actions by December 31, 2019, whereas financial service institutions collecting pension funds with the most assets – a minimum of one trillion rupiah – are required to deliver all documents by December 31, 2025.

2.3. Theoretical Perspective

To answer the first research question, "Have sustainable finance practices implemented by ABC Bank been consistent with the concept and framework of sustainable corporate finance?" A conceptual framework from Soppe (2004), which is rooted in ethics theory, is used as a part of the sustainable finance parameters. There are four parameters to answer four specific research questions: "Have sustainable finance practices implemented by ABC Bank been consistent with the theory of the firm, human nature of the economic actor, ownership paradigm, and ethical framework?"

The first parameter is the *theory of the firm*, which explains the fundamental reason a company was founded (Lozano, Carpenter, & Huisingh, 2015). The traditional finance concept goes with the private property rights model, which states that the firm as the owner of its assets should be allowed to use and allocate all of its assets for the sole purpose of gaining as much profit as possible (de Avila Monteiro & Zylbersztajn, 2012). The second parameter is the *human nature of the economic actor*. From a moral economic perspective, a sustainable finance-based firm, aside from its utility, enables it to also care about something else, such as the interests of other related parties, the well-being of people whose interests are at stake, its reputation, and its self-conception (Zsolnai, 2007).

The third parameter is *ownership paradigm*, a perspective that observes who exactly "owns" the firm. Sustainable finance agrees with stakeholder theory, which argues that a shareholder's interest should not be the only interest considered in a firm's decision-making because the firm should also consider the interest of every stakeholder (Sundaram & Inkpen, 2004). The last parameter is an *ethical framework*, a moral debate to decide what is good and right in business (Adhariani, Sciulli, & Clift, 2017). Sustainable finance agrees with the concept of virtue ethics, in which a firm should always undergo an internal push to act virtuously when conducting business (Soppe, 2004).

At the practical level, this research also uses another set of parameters to evaluate the implementation of sustainable finance using the parameters set by OJK, the Indonesia Financial Service Authority. The first parameter is the *implementation of eight sustainable finance principles*, a set of principles by OJK that acts as a guide to help firms integrate the concept of sustainable finance into their business operations. Only if a firm has successfully implemented these parameters can it be considered a sustainable finance firm. The parameters listed by OJK are as follows:

(a) responsible investment;
(b) strategy and sustainable business practice;
(c) social and environmental risk management;
(d) corporate governance;
(e) informative communication;
(f) inclusivity;
(g) development of superior and potential sector; and
(h) coordinative and collaborative.

The second parameter is the *preparation of a sustainable finance action plan*, a document containing the firm's business plan for the short (one year) and long term (five years) (Otoritas Jasa Keuangan, 2017). OJK through POJK 51 obliges the issuance of this action plan to ensure that every company has put maximum effort into implementing sustainable finance. This document is an additional document that complements the annual report and sustainability report by providing all information relevant to the firm's efforts in implementing sustainable finance. That said, the document should include at least the following content:

(a) executive summary;
(b) process of action plan preparation;
(c) determining factor of the action plan;
(d) priority and analysis of the action plan; and
(e) follow-up of the action plan.

The last parameter is the *preparation of sustainability report*. As previously mentioned, the sustainability report is issued to account for the firm's program from both social and environmental aspects (Mori, Best, & Cotter, 2014). OJK through POJK 51 obliges the issuance of a sustainability report for the first time because no regulation on sustainability reports has been previously issued, which has resulted in a very low level of sustainability report issuance in Indonesia. All issued sustainability reports should at least contain the following aspects:

(a) explanation of sustainability strategies;
(b) an overview of sustainability aspects;
(c) short profile of the firm;
(d) Statement of directors;
(e) governance of sustainability;
(f) sustainability performance;
(g) written verification from an independent party, if any;
(h) feedback sheet for the reader, if any; and
(i) firm's response to previous year's feedback, if any.

Based on the theoretical perspective, we develop our research framework, as depicted in Fig. 3.1.

2.4. Economic, Social, and Environmental Context of ABC

Since 2009, ABC has begun to apply the concept of sustainable finance through environment-friendly programs implemented internally. The programs contain values to increase awareness and responsibility for natural and

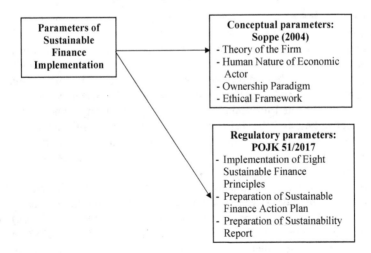

Fig. 3.1.   Research Framework.

social environments. The eco-friendly program has four components of sustainability: natural, social, human resources, and economics. These are used as a reference in business activities to produce products and services that are environment friendly. In addition to the program, ABC also has sustainability banking principles – a set of principles that govern ABC activities in all aspects, such as risk management, community development, bank operations, and corporate social responsibility.

As one of the largest financial services institutions in Indonesia, ABC started its sustainable financial implementation before the obligatory regulations because the bank believes that the implementation of sustainable finance is essential to survive fierce industry competition. Moreover, implementation of sustainable finance at ABC can also be a significant source of funding for long-term development in Indonesia. Through the implementation of sustainable finance, ABC will also fund environment-related projects, such as renewable energy electricity projects, to provide benefits to the community and the environment. These environment-friendly projects can prevent and reduce environmental damage and encourage efficient and environment-friendly energy use. Funding for other environment-friendly projects continues to increase. In 2017 alone, the amount of credit channeled to such projects was 30.66% of total corporate loans, up from 12.39% in 2016. These figures indicate that ABC's concern for the environment encourages companies to continue providing credit to environment-friendly projects that are expected to help not only the economy of the surrounding community but also the preservation of the environment.

3. RESEARCH METHOD

The case study method, a qualitative analysis, was used to analyze the implementation of sustainable finance at ABC. This method enables an in-depth and focused empirical investigation of a contemporary phenomenon in the real world (Yin, 2009). The choice of ABC as the sample is justified given its high commitment to sustainability issues. It is one of the largest financial service providers in Indonesia and one of the BUMN (SOEs) companies that listed its shares on the Indonesia Stock Exchange. Majority ownership is held by the government, and the rest is owned by the public. ABC also has several subsidiaries that support the provision of integrated financial services. The intended subsidiary is engaged in sharia securities, insurance, remittance, and multifinance.

Data were collected through semi-structured interviews, thematic analysis on the news of ABC sustainable finance in national online newspapers for 2015–2019 (including news containing interviews with ABC executives), and document analysis (annual and sustainability reports from 2015–2017 and the company's internal documents). The triangulation of data sources is expected to substantiate and enhance the validity of the research results because we were not able to conduct more interviews with key persons given the limited access provided by the company.

We interviewed two key persons at ABC who handled the planning and implementation of sustainability issues. They are part of a cross-division team that integrates the concept of sustainable finance with ABC Bank's operational activities. Details of the interviewees are provided in Table 3.1.

The first step of this research begins by identifying a set of questions to be used in the interviews. The questions are derived from theory and the related literature and are depicted in the table in the Appendix. The interviewees' responses, newspapers, and corporate reports and documents were examined through a qualitative content analysis (Krippendorff, 2018). Codes were generated by the authors from the analysis of various data and then mapped them with Soppe (2004) and the POJK framework. The narrative strategy for data analysis (Langley, 1999) was applied after reviewing and adjusting the coding. The use of Soppe (2004) and POJK framework guides us deductively in grouping the codes and their associated quotations into main categories according to the common themes (O'Dwyer, 2004) suggested by those frameworks. The document analysis helps us understand the reports produced by ABC as required by POJK 51, namely, the sustainable action plan and sustainability report. We constantly revisited the original data during the analysis to ensure that all statements from various sources were understood and properly applied in their original context (Cho, Laine, Roberts, & Rodrigue, 2015). Table 3.2 presents the data sources other than the interviews.

Table 3.1.   Interviewee Details.

Interviewee	Position	Job responsibilities	Management level
1	General Manager, Budgeting and Financial Control Division	Budget preparation, control of fund distributions (credit), financial transactions	Executive
2	Head of Financial Report Preparation	Accounting, financial reporting	Middle level

Table 3.2.   Non-interview Data Sources.

Type	Explanation
National online newspapers for the period 2015–2019	The news was searched through Google using the keyword "ABC sustainable finance 2015–2019." The search resulted in 10,100 articles. After careful selection by considering the relevance and duplication, only 40 articles were used in the analysis
Company's document analysis	Publicly available: – Annual report 2015, 2016, 2017 – Sustainability report 2015, 2016, 2017 ABC internal documents: – Shareholder Aspiration Letter – Sustainable Finance Action Plan

4. FINDINGS

4.1. Analysis of ABC Sustainable Finance Practices Using Soppe (2004) Parameters

In this section, ABC's business activities are analyzed to ultimately decide if their business operation has been in line with the parameters set by Soppe (2004). The first parameter to be analyzed is the *theory of the firm*. To be considered success-ful in fulfilling the first parameter, a firm must highlight its awareness that it was not founded solely to make profits. To address this concern, the first analysis is the reason a company is established. As an SOE, the reason for establishing SOEs is already regulated according to the applicable legislation, namely, the Law on State-owned Enterprises (No. 19/2003).

The existence of regulations for SOEs indicates that ABC as one of the SOEs already has a fundamental reason for implementing sustainable financial con-cepts. Such a regulation is a government effort to ensure that the making profit is not the firm's only goal. As mentioned by an interviewee:

> As an SOE, we are not only seeking profit but also [providing] added value for the tax and the state. This is about state-owned and non-SOEs. As a state-owned company we reach out to the remote areas which, if calculated economically only, it will be more profitable if we invest elsewhere such as in big cities or in cities that have high economic potential like what has been done by non-state-owned banks.

In addition to encouraging financial inclusion, ABC's concern for social and environmental aspects is also seen in the Partnership and Community Development Programme (PKBL) aimed at improving people's welfare and nature conservation. In this program, ABC actively helps SMEs grow and develop by providing low-interest rate loans and guidance and supervision to enable them to be self-sustaining and grow as a business. This partnership program is not binding in the sense that no compulsion exists for ABC's partners that have grown into customers, which is in accordance with the exposure of an interviewee:

> Actually, we also gain profit from the programme, but we first give them something. If they want to become our customer then it is so appreciated; otherwise, it is still okay. The term is not binding if the partners grow but later on they turned out to other parties, it is not a problem.

In a community development program, ABC cooperates with both local and international institutions with the same vision and commitment to create a sus-tainable world by contributing credit and funding to fund various environmental conservation programs. This program highlights ABC's efforts to improve peo-ple's living standards through ways that are in line with the concept of sustainable development.

This analysis shows that ABC has applied the concept of a triple bottom line, which is confirmed given that the success of ABC is no longer judged solely from the financial achievement but also its social and environmental perfor-mance. ABC's awareness of its social and environmental performance can also be seen from the publication of sustainability reports as a means for companies to account for the performance of social and environmental aspects so that the public can scrutinize and criticize its performance from both aspects. Doing so incentivizes firms to further achieve a higher standard of performance in terms of financial, social, and environmental aspects.

The second analysis concerns the *human nature of the economic actor*. Based on this parameter, a company must show that, in a decision-making process, a firm does not solely use profit as an absolute parameter. Instead, the firm should also consider the impact on other concerned parties.

To assess this parameter, the first factor to analyze is the company's business decision-making process. ABC has integrated the assessment of social and environmental impacts into its decision-making process. The firm crediting process is used as an example. When considering a credit application by a prospective client, ABC does not use the client's rate of return and financial capacity as the only determinant factor in the decision-making process. Instead, it also considers various risks that it and related parties must bear while also considering the impact of the client's business activities on social and environmental aspects, as stated by an interviewee:

> When a credit analyst recommends credit, he has considered financial projections, environmental risks, reputation risk, and duration of use. We consider the risk exposed to our bank. For example, if we give credit to a mining company with production [to] run for 10 years, we will think within the 10 years exploitation, what will be the cash flow to us as a creditor? This includes cash flow to cope with the costs to restore the environmental impact.

To implement this parameter, ABC developed the Corporate Banking Credit Guideline Book I, a credit requirement for its prospective customers to ensure that the credit decision also considers customers' efforts to preserve the environment and their responsibility for all possible environmental and social impacts. This is done by requiring prospective customers to include documents such as Analysis on Environmental Impact (AMDAL) in their credit applications. Specifically, for companies with the potential to have a significant impact on the environment, ABC will also only process their application if they pass their Environmental Performance Rating Programme by the Ministry of Environment and Forestry, an assessment of the company's compliance with the applicable environmental regulations in Indonesia. ABC will only process applications of companies categorized as blue, green, or gold, indicating that they have proven that they comply with all regulations relevant to their respective business activities.

ABC would also oblige prospective clients from several industries to provide an industry-specific requirement. For instance, prospective clients from the palm oil industry should also be certified by RSPO and ISPO for their credit application to be processed further. Using these various standards in the credit application process, it can be concluded that ABC has highlighted its concern over the impact of its actions on other parties – something that became one of the characteristics of a moral economic man.

The third parameter is the *ownership paradigm*. A successful application of this parameter can be reflected in a company's understanding that shareholders' interests cannot be the only interest on which a firm's decision is based. Companies that implement sustainable finance understand the interests of all stakeholders and strive to meet their interests as well.

To assess this parameter, the first analysis is of the company's vision statement. Based on the 2017 financial statements, ABC's vision is to become a financial institution that excels in service and performance. From the firm vision statement previously mentioned, ABC is not solely focused on the fulfillment of shareholders' interests. This view is evident from the company's vision statement, which clearly states that one of the company's goals is to create added value for stakeholders. As an interviewee puts it:

> We had a review when we revised the vision in 2014, we've put everything there, from the political, economic, social, technological, environmental, and legal. We have performed the adequate study, and we describe it also to management. In developing the vision, we also have inquired parties involved.

Although ABC Bank has consistently used a stakeholder theory approach to meet the interests of all stakeholders, it also recognizes that when there is a conflict of interest among stakeholders, ABC always prioritizes the interests of shareholders. Although this is seen as a form of application of shareholder theory, what needs to be underlined is the ownership structure of ABC, which is different from private companies. In a state-owned company, the dividing line between the interests of shareholders and stakeholders is not very clear. This is because most of the shares are owned by the Indonesian government, which indirectly represents the interests of the general public. The decision of ABC Bank to continue to prioritize the interests of the government is due to the basic assumption that the government will always represent the interests of the community. Therefore, ABC Bank's decision to prioritize shareholders' interests in the event of a conflict of interest can indirectly help meet the interests of the general public as well. This is in accordance with the statement of an interviewee:

> The problem is that our shareholders are the State, and the State represents the People's Consultative Assembly, the People's Legislative Assembly and the Parliament and the President along with his staff. So, the focus of ABC Bank is to prioritize the interests of the State, that's all. State is the Government, and the Government must carry out the mandate of the public, right?

The last parameter is the *ethical framework*. This parameter requires the company to use virtue ethics theory as the basis of moral judgment regarding its decision – that is, the company engages in virtuous behavior because of the internal push to become a virtuous company and not because of existing regulations. Several ABC policies highlight its characteristic as a company that implements virtue ethics. For example, ABC has shown its awareness as part of a larger community and played its role in society, which is reflected in an interviewee's opinion:

> We see ABC as part of a society with their own respective functions. Yes, we also have our function. So, we cannot carry out the function of others. If we carry out our function well, then the business or society will also run well.

ABC has actively encouraged its employees to behave virtuously in both business and daily life contexts. For that, ABC has compiled two guides, the Code of Conduct and company principles. The ABC Code of Conduct contains 14 points that regulate the relationship between its employees and all stakeholders regarding conducting business activities. Meanwhile, the company's principle is that a work culture and behavior are expected from all employees. This guidance has also become the basis of ABC encouraging all employees – from its board of directors, management, and employees in general – to always behave virtuously.

Assessing the implementation of sustainable finance at ABC with all the parameters set by Soppe (2004) we can conclude that ABC has implemented the concept of sustainable finance. This conclusion is the result of the analysis of the entire set of parameters, indicating that ABC has applied the concept of sustainable finance based on the set of parameters set by Soppe (2004).

4.2. Analysis of ABC Sustainable Finance Practices Using POJK 51 Parameters

Aside from using the parameters set by Soppe (2004), this study also analyzes ABC's preparation in applying sustainable financial concepts under the Regulation of the Financial Services Authority Number 51/POJK.03/2017 for financial service institutions, issuers, and public companies. OJK uses three parameters: implementation of eight sustainable financial principles, the preparation of a sustainable finance action plan, and the preparation of sustainability reports. This section mostly attempts to assess ABC's preparation process to face the guidelines in POJK 51 because ABC is preparing the implementation of POJK 51 and will apply it during 2019. This applies to all aspects except the preparation of sustainability reports that have been done by ABC even before POJK 51 is legalized.

The first parameter to be analyzed is the *implementation of* the eight sustainable finance principles. All this time, ABC has implemented the concept of sustainable finance even without existence of a regulation for it. The initiative was performed to accommodate several projects with sustainability aspects embedded in the requirements. Since 2009, ABC also uses some guidelines when implementing sustainable finance, such as the use of Global Reporting Initiative (GRI) standards to prepare sustainability reports, the standards of responsible investment in the credit application process, and stakeholder engagement to determine the firm's CSR program target. Although ABC has implemented various aspects of sustainable finance, its implementation has not been as integrated as POJK 51 expected, as also stated by an interviewee:

> I'm sure everything is there but has not been structured as expected in the POJK. For example, the principle responsible investment, it is all about the portfolio, right? Actually, we have already had risk management put in our portfolio which set the investment guidance in certain industrial sectors. I think we have already implemented it, only reporting in such form that is not.

The second parameter is the preparation of a *sustainable finance action plan*. This plan is an entirely new document required by OJK that must be prepared by all financial service institutions in Indonesia. ABC is now entering the early preparation stage to develop an action plan. In the previous section, the task force team also plays a major role in preparing the action plan because one of the main outputs of the cross-division team is the company's action plan structured based on the POJK 51 regulations. The action plan itself must be issued by the company on December 31, 2019.

The last parameter to be evaluated is the preparation of the *sustainability report*. ABC is the first state-owned bank in Indonesia to issue a GRI-based sustainability report. Since 2009, ABC has consistently issued sustainability reports as separate from the annual reports. This effort is a form of transparency over efforts to realize the company's vision and face sustainability challenges. This sustainability report is structured as per GRI G4 standards and guidelines using in-accordance rules by selecting core options through which this report contains essential elements.

ABC's sustainability report is published through the company's official website to facilitate public access to the information. Prior to publication, ABC's sustainability report is checked and verified by a third party to ensure compliance with the standards used. In 2016, ABC's sustainability report was reviewed by NCSR, an independent organization focused on the implementation and proliferation of sustainable finance concepts in Indonesia. In 2017, ABC's sustainability report was reviewed by SR Asia, a nonprofit international organization that provides testing services for compliance with GRI sustainability reports and AccountAbility AA1000 standards, a company performance assessment standard for the company's accountability and sustainable development aspects.

4.3. Sustainable Finance Implementation Challenges

This section is attributed to answer the second research question: "What are challenges faced by ABC Bank in implementing sustainable finance?" The results show that ABC faced two challenges when applying the concept of sustainable finance. The first problem was the absence of a benchmark to use as guidance when preparing the report, as noted by an interviewee:

> The obstacles in Indonesia is that there is no benchmark. If there is one then it would be easier, as we do not have to find out by ourselves because it does not guarantee the best practice. There is no good example yet, and the guidance is only from the regulation. The concept is there, but we are still confused as we have no experiences in that matter.

RAKB is a document that was never previously compiled in Indonesia, and the absence of documents can be used as a guide – enough to inhibit the preparation process of RAKB by ABC. ABC has been using only POJK 51 and its attachments and explanations as a guide. However, with limited POJK 51 guidance, this first draft of the RAKB is the result of ABC's interpretation and understanding of the newly enacted POJK 51.

The second problem faced by the company is internal ABC employees' low understanding of the concept of sustainable finance. Their understanding is not comprehensive. Only certain divisions understand the concept of sustainable finance, so implementing sustainable finance that requires the joint effort of all parties and related divisions within the company is difficult. To solve all these problems, ABC establishes an intensive communication with OJK to ensure that the interpretation used by ABC toward POJK 51 is an interpretation expected by OJK. Moreover, ABC also establishes communication with WWF-Indonesia for guidance and supervision when drafting the action plan. Moreover,

WWF-Indonesia frequently conducts training for ABC employees to develop the bank's internal competence in sustainable finance.

5. DISCUSSION AND CONCLUSION

This study offers a good news story as a practical contribution – the implementation of sustainable finance in a state-owned bank in Indonesia. This study also adds to existing cases that have explored the incorporation of sustainability into business practices (Hopwood, Unerman, & Fries, 2010). The findings show that although almost ideal, the implementation was still problematic at the operational level because the profitability objective needed to be achieved. As an agent of the government, this bank aims to balance the goals of public welfare and economic motives by empowering the community and preserving the environment through its credit distribution activities. The concept of sustainable finance has been applied at ABC through several practices grounded in the awareness of public interest long before such an application became mandatory through regulation in Indonesia. This indicates that in the context of Indonesia as a developing country, the implementation of sustainable finance is still driven by regulation. The implementation can serve as a benchmark for other institutions seeking the adoption of sustainable finance as mandated by Indonesia regulation under POJK 51/2017. In the academic field, prior to formal regulation, less is known about sustainable finance implementation in the context of Indonesia; hence, the topic was understudied but is expected to flourish in future.

The framework offered in this study using the Soppe (2004) and POJK 51 parameters serves as the theoretical and practical contributions. In general, the analysis shows that ABC implemented the concept and practice of sustainable finance. The triple-bottom-line concept has been adopted because the company acknowledged that it is not founded solely to gain profit but also to improve social welfare, preserve the environment, and contribute to development in Indonesia. This is done through additional requirements for future creditors to show that the proposed activities to be financed are not detrimental to the environment. This implies that in the decision-making process, the company considers the impact of its business decisions on society and the environment alongside its economic rationale.

In addition to stockholder aspiration, several guidelines regulating a bank's operations have become the rules of practice. Prior to POJK 51, ABC has internal guidelines to support the implementation of sustainable finance. To implement the eight sustainable finance principles, ABC has established a task force team that identifies the shortcomings of the ongoing implementation of sustainable finance at ABC and makes the necessary adjustments in accordance with the OJK sustainable financial roadmap and POJK 51. When preparing a sustainable finance action plan, ABC has also established communication with third parties. Given the absence of benchmarks that ABC can use as guides when drafting the action plan, the bank has actively engaged in communication and working with OJK and WWF-Indonesia for guidance during the drafting process. To comply with the expected sustainability report requirements in POJK 51, ABC has also adjusted the sustainability report. Given that no regulations exist to officially regulate the structure of the sustainability report for financial services institutions in Indonesia, ABC is currently adjusting its sustainability report to the provisions of POJK 51.

To summarize, the activities that constitute sustainable finance practices at ABC Bank are likely to be organized by: (1) understanding – practical and general understandings of the sustainable finance concept; how to collect, analyze, summarize, and make sense of information to support the implementation; and what information to use and communicate to stakeholders; (2) rules and principles – regulations on sustainability and sustainable finance in Indonesia, guidelines on conducting/disseminating the progress of implementation, shared norms, and ethical considerations to understand company best practice stories; and (3) practical structure – a structure that embraces normative ends such as the adequate and timely reporting required by the regulation, efficient gathering of sustainability information prior to credit approval, and acceptable uses of financing policies to support sustainability.

The consistency of the conceptual framework of Soppe (2004) implies that OJK and other stakeholders can use the framework to evaluate the implementation of sustainable finance in an institution. The institution itself can use the framework to evaluate their readiness for the implementation of sustainable finance in their internal operations.

Based on these findings, the most significant challenge to the implementation of sustainable finance at ABC is the lack of skilled employees who understand the concept of sustainable finance comprehensively, so that difficulties do not exist in the interpretation of POJK 51 and in translating the concept into corporate practices. As stated by Strandberg (2005) and Jabbour and Santos (2008), employees play a significant role in sustainable finance; hence the lack of knowledgeable employees implies that OJK as the regulator needs to provide continuous socialization and training to enhance the understanding of the concept. Given its improved performance in sustainable finance, ABC can become the benchmark for other financial service institutions to implement sustainable finance in Indonesia. This goal is certainly in line with ABC Bank's vision to become a financial service institution that excels in service and performance.

Another implication for the regulator comes from the fact that ABC's sustainable finance implementation is highly driven by its status as a state-owned bank with dual missions of public interest and profits. This implies the need for substantial involvement from the government (Feitelson, 1992) through regulations and operational guidelines, especially for other institutions with other ownership types. To support this notion, users of financial reporting must be educated to give them more sustainable awareness of the operations of banks and other companies to form a market and stakeholder demand for sustainable finance. This is particularly important for small banks (identified as BUKU 1 and 2 in Indonesia) as the implementation of sustainable finance (which is targeted to be in 2020 for small banks) can conflict with credit distribution to smaller creditors with little understanding of sustainable finance. The implementation of sustainable finance in small banks can negatively impact the performance as they have to add human resources, increase the capacity of the existing employees, and perform socialization programs for all employees, which require additional costs and can increase the ratio of banks' operational expenses to operational revenues. In the Indonesian context, this can be a pressure for small banks to consolidate. In the global context, this can imply a significant amount of funds needed from developed countries to support the development of sustainable finance in Indonesia, especially to encourage implementation by small banks.

Subsequent research can analyze comparisons in the implementation of sustainable finance between financial service institutions in Indonesia and other countries that are more experienced with such implementations and already have adequate regulations. Such comparison can indicate the gap between the application of sustainable finance in Indonesia and the best practices of other countries. Further research can also analyze more than one financial service institution in Indonesia to understand the general trends in motivation and the challenges to the implementation of sustainable finance in Indonesia. Further research can also conduct a longitudinal analysis to substantiate the findings from this early phase of sustainable finance implementation, in particular to evaluate whether the true motive remains the same or other factors from societal and institutional pressures divert it to become a "pseudo" motive of sustainable finance given the organized hypocrisy and organizational facades, as indicated by Cho et al. (2015) for the sustainability reporting case.

REFERENCES

Adhariani, D., Sciulli, N., & Clift, R. (2017). *Financial management and corporate governance from the feminist ethics of care perspective*. Cham: Palgrave Macmillan.

Banga, J. (2019). The green bond market: A potential source of climate finance for developing countries. *Journal of Sustainable Finance & Investment, 9*(1), 17–32.

Cash, D. (2017). Sustainable finance: Why the formal introduction of credit rating agencies should serve as a warning. Retrieved from https://ssrn.com/abstract=3007701. Accessed on October 12, 2020.

Cho, C. H., Laine, M., Roberts, R. W., & Rodrigue, M. (2015). Organized hypocrisy, organizational façades, and sustainability reporting. *Accounting, Organizations and Society, 40*, 78–94.

de Avila Monteiro, G. F., & Zylbersztajn, D. (2012). A property rights approach to strategy. *Strategic Organization, 10*(4), 366–383.

Feitelson, E. (1992). An alternative role for economic instruments: Sustainable finance for environmental management. *Environmental Management, 16*(3), 299–307.

Forcadell, F. J., & Aracil, E. (2017). Sustainable banking in Latin American developing countries: Leading to (mutual) prosperity. *Business Ethics: A European Review, 26*(4), 382–395.

Goldenberg, S. (2015). Indonesia to cut carbon emissions by 29% by 2030. *The Guardian: International Edition*, 24 September, p. 1.

Hopwood, A., Unerman, J., & Fries, J. (Eds.). (2010). *Accounting for sustainability: Practical insights*. London: Routledge.

Jabbour, C. J. C., & Santos, F. C. A. (2008). The central role of human resource management in the search for sustainable organizations. *The International Journal of Human Resource Management, 19*(12), 2133–2154.

Jeucken, M. (2010). *Sustainable finance and banking: The financial sector and the future of the planet*. London: Routledge.

Jeucken, M., & Bouma, J. (2017). The changing environment of banks. M. Jeucken & J. Bouma, (Eds.), *Sustainable banking* (pp. 24–38). London: Routledge.

Kaptein, M., & Wempe, J. (2002). *The balanced company: A theory of corporate integrity*. Oxford: Oxford University Press.

Klein, P. G., Mahoney, J. T., McGahan, A. M., & Pitelis, C. N. (2012). Who is in charge? A property rights perspective on stakeholder governance. *Strategic Organization, 10*(3), 304–315.

Krippendorff, K. (2018). *Content analysis: An introduction to its methodology*. California, IL: Sage Publications.

Langley, A. (1999). Strategies for theorizing from process data. *Academy of Management Review, 24*(4), 691–710.

Lan, L. L., & Heracleous, L. (2010). Rethinking agency theory: The view from law. *Academy of Management Review, 35*(2), 294–314.

Lozano, R., Carpenter, A., & Huisingh, D. (2015). A review of "theories of the firm" and their contributions to corporate sustainability. *Journal of Cleaner Production, 106*(1), 430–442.

Mori, R., Best, P., & Cotter, J. (2014). Sustainability reporting and assurance: A historical analysis of a world-wide phenomenon. *Journal of Business Ethics, 120*(1), 1–11.

O'Dwyer, B. (2004). Qualitative data analysis: Illuminating a process for transforming a "messy" but "attractive" "nuisance." In C. Humphrey & B. Lee (Eds.), *The real life guide to accounting research: A behind-the-scene view of using qualitative research methods* (pp. 391–407). London: Elsevier.

Otoritas Jasa Keuangan [Financial Services Authority] (2017). Peraturan Otoritas Jasa Keuangan Nomor 51/POJK.03/2017 tentang Penerapan Keuangan Berkelanjutan Bagi Lembaga Jasa Keuangan, Emiten, dan Perusahaan Publik [Regulation of the Financial Services Authority No. 51/POJK.03/2017 on the Application of Sustainable Finance for Financial Services Institutions, Issuers and Public Companies].

Schaltegger, S., Hörisch, J., & Freeman, R. E. (2017). Business cases for sustainability: A stakeholder theory perspective. *Organization & Environment, 32*(3), 191–212. https://doi.org/10.1177/1086026617722882

Soppe, A. (2004). Sustainable corporate finance. *Journal of Business Ethics, 53*(1–2), 213–224.

Srinivas, P. S., & Sitorus, D. (2004, April). The role of state-owned banks in Indonesia. In *Financial markets and development conference*. Washington, DC: World Bank and IMF.

Strandberg, C. (2005). The future of sustainable finance: Thought leaders study. Retrieved from https://corostrandberg.com/wp-content/uploads/2005/12/sustainable-finance-future-trends.pdf. Accessed on June 2, 2020.

Sundaram, A. K., & Inkpen, A. C. (2004). The corporate objective revisited. *Organization Science, 15*(3), 350–363.

Yin, R. K. (2009). *Case study research: Design and methods (Vol. 5)*. Thousand Oaks, CA: Sage Publications.

Zsolnai, L. (2007). The moral economic man. In L. Zsolnai, (Ed.), *Ethics in the economy* (pp. 39–58). New York, NY: Peter Lang Publishing Group in association with GSE Research.

APPENDIX: LIST OF QUESTIONS FOR INTERVIEWEES

No.	Questions	Justifications	Source
	1. Can PT ABC be considered when applying the sustainable financial concept based on the Soppe (2004) parameter?		
	Theory of the firm		
1	What are ABC's vision and mission?	To explore the objective of the firm, whether it is only profit oriented or any trace of awareness exists for the environmental and social aspect accommodated in the vision and mission statement	Soppe (2004)
2	Which party interests are considered in composing the vision and mission of ABC?	To investigate the perspective adopted in the vision and mission: shareholder versus stakeholder	Soppe (2004)
3	Do you think that social and environment also play a role in achieving the planned performance?	To investigate the level of awareness of ABC executives of the contributions of external parties in the achievement of the company's objectives	Soppe (2004)
4	Does ABC feel any responsibility other than to increase the value of the company?	To determine whether PT ABC feels that increasing the company's value is the sole responsibility that PT ABC owns or feels that other responsibilities must also be met	Soppe (2004)
5	Does ABC have a specific program to provide value to the social and environment?	To understand what ABC has done to provide benefits to the surrounding environment (both natural and social environment)	Soppe (2004)
6	Has ABC actively used the triple-bottom-line approach to have achievement targets in: – Financial aspect – Environmental aspects – Social aspects	To determine whether PT ABC has implemented a triple-bottom-line approach that not only makes financial achievement the sole parameter of a company's success	Soppe (2004)
	Human nature of the economic actor		
7	Are ABC's business decisions only based on the profit to be obtained? – If yes, why? – If not, what is the basis of ABC's business decision? This question is asked to understand whether PT ABC has the characteristics of an organization that can be categorized as homo economicus – characterized by its selfish and rational nature	To understand whether ABC has the characteristics of an organization that can be categorized as homo economicus – characterized by its selfish and rational nature	Soppe (2004)
8	Does ABC consider the impact to other parties in any business decisions taken? Can you give an example?	To understand whether ABC has the characteristics of an organization that can be categorized as a Moral Economic Man – characterized by its caring nature toward other parties affected by its economic activities	Zsolnai (2007)

(Continued)

(Continued)

No.	Questions	Justifications	Source
9	Will ABC be willing to lower its profitability to provide more value to others? Can you give an example?	To understand whether ABC has the characteristics of an organization that can be categorized as Moral Economic Man – characterized by its willingness to reduce the satisfaction/profits to increase the benefits of others about whom he cares	Zsolnai (2007)
10	Does PT ABC care about the public image arising from its business decisions?	To understand whether ABC has the characteristics of an organization that can be categorized as Moral Economic Man – characterized by the nature of caring about the views of others regarding economic decisions made.	Zsolnai (2007)
11	Does ABC have its ideals as to what a company should be?	To understand whether ABC has the characteristics of an organization that can be categorized as Moral Economic Man – characterized by its nature that survives on its idealism about the ideal organizational character	Zsolnai (2007)
Ownership paradigm			
12	According to ABC, who are the parties entitled to benefit gained by ABC?	To understand the views of ABC on which party the residual claimant is actually entitled to benefit from ABC	Lan and Heracleous (2010)
13	According to ABC, who are the stakeholders involved in business activities?	To understand the views of ABC on which parties are considered to correlate (impact) with all of its business activities	Soppe (2004)
14	Do you think that all stakeholders support the success of ABC's business activities?	To understand whether ABC is aware of the contributions from stakeholders	Soppe (2004)
15	How does ABC understand the interests of stakeholders other than shareholders?	To understand the way ABC gained an understanding of stakeholder interests	Klein et al. (2012)
16	Has ABC prioritized decision-making on the interests of shareholders over the interests of other parties and vice versa?	To understand whether the decision-making is based on the shareholder or stakeholder approach	Klein et al. (2012)
Ethical framework			
17	What ethical approach is used by ABC in business decision-making?	To understand the ethical approach used (utilitarian, right, justice, or caring)	Adhariani et al. (2017)
	a. Decision-making is based on the impact of such a decision	The assessment of the utilitarian approach	
	b. Correct decision-making is a decision not imposed by others	The assessment of the right approach	

(Continued)

(Continued)

No.	Questions	Justifications	Source
	c. Correct decision-making is a decision that does not negatively impact the other parties	The appraisal of the justice approach	
	d. Correct decision-making is decision-making that considers good relationships with others	The assessment of a caring approach	
18	Does ABC consider itself a moral entity responsible for its business activities? Could you please provide an example?	To determine whether ABC considers that it or management – as the individual making the decision – is accountable for every business decision	Kaptein and Wempe (2002)
19	Does ABC use morality considerations in business decision-making? If so, is there an example of such a decision?	To determine whether ABC tends to adopt a "business is business" or "virtuous ethics" approach that considers morality in business decision making	Kaptein and Wempe (2002)
20	Does ABC have any social obligations arising from existence as a financial services institution?	To understand whether ABC feels that a social responsibility arises from the existence of ABC as a company or whether the responsibility is limited to earning profits for shareholders' interests	Kaptein and Wempe (2002)
21	Does ABC feel it has become a virtuous company?	To assess whether ABC tends to apply virtue ethics using the six parameters in Solomon (2004)	Solomon (2004)
	a. Does ABC in decision-making see itself as an institution only or as part of the broader community?	Assessment of the dimensions of community	
	b. Does ABC only perform compliance to the minimum level against applicable regulations or has it gone the extra mile for what it considers important?	Assessment of the dimensions of excellence	
	c. Does ABC have a code of ethics specific to a particular position or does it only have a code of ethics common to all employees?	Assessment of the dimensions of role identity	
	d. Does ABC have a program/activity to improve the integrity of employees?	Assessment of the dimensions of integrity	
	e. Does the ethical decision-making of ABC always refer to the applicable regulations or does it sometimes use management's judgement?	Assessment of the dimensions of good judgement	
	f. Is a person's ethics one of the assessments of employee acceptance at ABC?	Assessment of the dimensions of holism	

(Continued)

(Continued)

No.	Questions	Justifications	Source
	2. Can ABC be considered to apply a sustainable financial concept based on the related Indonesian Regulation (POJK – the regulation from the Authority of Financial Services)?		
22	a. Has ABC implemented the following principles:	This question is asked to assess the application of ABC's ongoing financial concepts using the parameters set by POJK 51	POJK Nomor 51/POJK.03/2017
	– Responsible investment principles	What is meant by "responsible investment principle" is a financial investment approach on sustainable development projects and initiatives, nature conservation products and policies that support sustainable economic development and believe that the creation of long-term investment benefits depend on the economic, social system, environment, and governance?	Explanation to POJK 51/POJK.03/2017
	– Principles of sustainable business strategy and practice	The "principles of sustainable business strategy and practice" is the development of value for the financial services sector to contribute to society through business policies and practices and the implementation of business strategies by financial services institutions, issuers and public companies by minimizing negative impacts and integrating the economic, social, environmental, and governance aspects of each sector and strategy of each line of business	Explanation to POJK 51/POJK.03/2017
	– Principles of social and environmental risk management	The term "principles of social and environmental risk management" is the integration of aspects of social responsibility and the protection and management of the environment in risk management to avoid, prevent, and minimize negative impacts arising from risk exposure related to social and environmental aspects	Explanation to POJK 51/POJK.03/2017
	– Governance principles	What is meant by "governance principles" is the application of governance to aspects of social responsibility and protection and management of the environment that are transparent, accountable, responsible, independent, equal and reasonable	Explanation to POJK 51/POJK.03/2017

(Continued)

(Continued)

No.	Questions	Justifications	Source
	– Informative communication principles	What is meant by "informative communication principles" is the use of appropriate communication models related to organizational strategy, governance, performance, and business prospects to all stakeholders	Explanation to POJK 51/POJK.03/2017
	– Inclusive principles	An "inclusive principle" refers to the equitable access of financial services institutions' products and/or services, issuers and public companies to the public, and to the entire territory of the Unitary State of the Republic of Indonesia to accelerate economic progress, social welfare, and environmental protection, communities that have not or at least have access to the institutions' products and/or services, issuers and public companies	Explanation to POJK 51/POJK.03/2017
	– Principles of priority sector development	Priority sector development principles aim to provide a larger portion of the priority sectors to achieve sustainable development goals, including mitigation and adaptation to climate change	Explanation to POJK 51/POJK.03/2017
	– Coordination and collaboration principles	The meaning of the "coordination and collaboration principle" is the enhancement of the coordination and collaboration of all stakeholders of the financial services sector, including ministries, institutions, sectors or business units that have programs closely linked to the implementation of sustainable development to accelerate the improvement of economic prosperity, social and environmental quality for all Indonesian people and to encourage community participation related to economic, social, environment, and governance aspects	Explanation to POJK 51/POJK.03/2017
23	What is ABC's motivation to intend to apply the concept of sustainable finance?	This question was asked to determine the fundamental reasons for ABC applying the concept of sustainable finance	All subsequent questions are developed by researchers

(Continued)

(Continued)

No.	Questions	Justifications	Source
	a. Is there a motivation to maintain a balance of public interest and to gain profits in sustainable financial implementation decisions?	To understand whether the implementation of sustainable finance in ABC is based on a profit or a social motive	
	b. If there is no POJK 51, will ABC continue to implement sustainable finance?	To explore whether sustainable financial implementation at ABC is due to awareness arising from the internal company or as a response to regulations issued by the regulator	
24	Has ABC been familiar with POJK 51?	This question is asked to determine the level of understanding of ABC against POJK 51 as a regulation that specifically regulates the application of the concept of sustainable finance at financial services agencies in Indonesia	
25	What activities have been done in response to POJK 51?	This question is asked to determine all of the preparations that ABC has made in fulfilling the obligations arising out of the legalization of POJK 51	
26	What preparation been made by ABC in preparing the sustainable financial action plan?	This question is asked to understand the latest developments by ABC in the preparation of the sustainable financial action plan required by the POJK 51 as a criterion for the implementation of sustainable finance	
27	What are the obstacles faced to comply with the provisions of the ongoing financial implementation in POJK 51?	This question is asked to identify barriers and obstacles faced by ABC in the effort to implement sustainable finance under the provisions stipulated in POJK 51	
28	Does ABC get external assistance in fulfilling the POJK 51 provisions?	This question is asked to determine whether support/assistance from external parties exists, from either the regulator or another third party	
29	What efforts will be done by ABC in tackling the existing problems?	This question is asked to understand ABC's future plan in the implementation of sustainable finance	

CHAPTER 4

HOW GREEN IS GREEN BANKING? AN ANALYSIS OF SLACK AND GREEN PRACTICES IN THE BANKING INDUSTRY

Malisa Salsabila and Desi Adhariani

ABSTRACT

This research analyzes the green activities implemented by banks in Indonesia following a new regulation on sustainable finance and the role of slack resources to fund the initiatives. Green practices of 35 banks in 2020–2021 were evaluated through the disclosure using green banking disclosure index (GBDI). The results show that the green practices have been disclosed adequately; however, no significant association was found for the role of financial and potential slack resources. This reflects the facts that the green activities might not have been adequately implemented and the organization's resources might not have been allocated to support the green practices. The research periods that were still overloaded with COVID-19 issue might hinder the banks from the adequate and appropriate allocation of resources toward green practices. This research recommends a prioritization approach for the implementation of the sustainable finance regulation by banks and authorities through the increased implementation of substantive green practices, not only the increased disclosures.

Keywords: Green banking; slack resources; sustainable finance; bank; disclosure index; Indonesia

Contemporary Issues in Financial Economics: Evidence from Emerging Economies
Research in Finance, Volume 37, 63–79
Copyright © 2023 by Emerald Publishing Limited
All rights of reproduction in any form reserved
ISSN: 0196-3821/doi:10.1108/S0196-382120230000037004

1. INTRODUCTION

The National Aeronautics and Space Administration (NASA) has provided a warning that the earth's surface is significantly warming; currently, in the last 2,000 years, the global temperature has been the highest. This is also supported by the literature in the field of sustainability related to climate change (de Oliveira & Jabbour, 2017; Tang & Demeritt, 2018; Whiteman, Walker, & Perego, 2013), which causes an increase in temperature, so preventive measures are needed to prevent sustainable effects (Figge & Hahn, 2013; Jones, 2010).

Preventive actions lead to incentives aimed at companies to contribute to green accounting or green business operations (van Liempd & Busch, 2013), including banks (Sun et al., 2020), which in turn aims to achieve sustainable development. Identical to the 3P concept, which refers to people, planet, and profit (Elkinjton, 1988), a company that runs with sustainable development means participating in repairing environmental damage, restoring biodiversity, habitat, and global warming (Jones, 2010).

Banks are major players in financial markets that are getting stronger at the global level. They must substantially reduce activities that have a negative impact on the environment (Hossain & Binte Rab, 2015). Banking efforts in sustainability development are realized through the concept of green banking (Bose, Khan, Rashid, & Islam, 2018; Miah, Rahman, & Mamoon, 2021), which is supported by POJK No. 51 of 2017 which requires the constitution of financial services (including banks), issuers, and public companies to disclose their activities through sustainability reports. Indonesia has also launched the Sustainable Finance Roadmap 2015–2019 requiring the formal financial sectors (banking, non-bank financial institutions, and capital markets) to contribute to national commitments in overcoming climate change. In order to achieve this, banks are required to develop action plans for sustainable financing and reporting (Financial Services Authority, 2020). This has had a positive impact on Indonesia which is categorized in the "Established" stage according to the International Finance Corporation (IFC), which means that Indonesia has comprehensive implementation actions and has started reporting the results and impacts of its commitment to sustainable finance. The complete IFC's assessment of the sustainable finance stage is depicted in Fig. 4.1.

Basically, banks need budgets and resources, which are obtained from slack resources, to carry out social and environmental obligations (Islam, Ghosh, & Khatun, 2021). The remaining cash or cash equivalents owned by banks is called financial slack (Zhang, Li, et al., 2018) which can be allocated to green banking activities, given that there are policies that require banks to report sustainability reports (Bose, Khan, & Monem, 2021; Wen, Lee, & Zhou, 2021). Like companies, banks also need other sources of funds to finance their activities (Godoy-Bejarano, Ruiz-Pava, & Téllez-Falla, 2020), which are obtained from external companies, such as debt issuance. The existence of unused debt capacity, called potential slack (Kim, Lee, Wi, & Lee, 2017; Kim, Shin, Shin, & Park, 2019), is expected to be used efficiently to support green banking practices.

The concept of green banking is closely related to corporate social responsibility (CSR; Dewi & Dewi, 2017), where both activities are nonfinancial activities

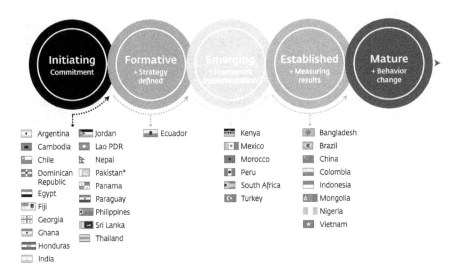

Fig. 4.1.   IFC's Assessment of the Sustainable Banking Network (SBN) in Sustainable Finance. *Source*: SBN Global Progress, IFC, 2018.

that care about the environment and need to be disclosed. CSR is how a company plays an active role in protecting the environment, while green banking is how a company (bank) runs its business in accordance with the concept of green business. The practice of green banking has several indicators to implement, and some of them are costly (the use of ATMs, m-banking, internet banking, SMS banking, and paperless), thus requiring resources to support the practice (Dwaikat & Ali, 2016; Mehedi & Kuddus, 2017).

Recent research related to green banking has focused on its relationship with the suitability of Islamic principles in driving green banking growth among green Muslim consumers (Bukhari, Hashim, Amran, & Hyder, 2020; Worden et al., 2017), implementation costs (Dwaikat & Ali, 2016), the effect of green products (Ongena, Peydró, & van Horen, 2015; Zhao, Li, Song, Li, & Wu, 2018), environmental sustainability development (Gliedt, Hoicka, & Jackson, 2018; Lavrinenko, Ignatjeva, Ohotina, Rybalkin, & Lazdans, 2019), financial performance (Bose et al., 2021; Hossain, Hossain, Rahman, & Karim, 2020; Julia & Kassim, 2020), and governance mechanisms (Bose et al., 2018). In their research, Mehedi and Kuddus (2017) present empirical evidence related to the application of green banking in Dutch–Bangla Banks and Italy (Falcone & Sica, 2019). In the context of Indonesia, Safitri, Hartiwiningsih, and Purwadi (2019) investigated the role of Indonesian law in the implementation of green banking, and its role in increasing operational cost efficiency (Pusva & Herlina, 2017), as well as the relationship between CSR and going concern (Dewi & Dewi, 2017). Recent literature on slack resources, particularly financial slack, focuses on its relationship to CSR performance (Zhang, Li, et al., 2018), CSR, sustainability, and integrated reporting (Kim et al., 2019), and firms' energy-saving behavior (Zhang, Wei, & Zhou, 2018). Meanwhile, potential slack focuses on its relationship with firm performance (Kim et al., 2017) and environmental complexity (Godoy-Bejarano et al., 2020). Based on the research above, there are still limited studies that focus empirically on the relationship between green banking and slack resources, which become the research gap that motivates this study.

In accordance with the legitimacy theory, the green banking activities imply that the bank has operated in accordance with social norms, maintains a good corporate image, and maintains legitimacy. This will have an impact on the credibility of the information that can affect the bank's prospects in the future when facing competitions over resources as predicted by signaling theory. Furthermore, stakeholder theory states that green banking can bring tangible benefits and fulfill stakeholder interests, so that it can help stakeholder decision-making more effective.

Like CSR, green banking has the opportunity to use slack resources owned by banks. This is a research question that looks at whether financial and potential slack have an effect on green banking, considering that becoming green is a new task for banks, hence it is only natural that the two slack will help them practice green banking. The latest regulation in Indonesia from the Authority of Financial Services, POJK No. 51 of 2017, states that Commercial Banks based on Business Activities (BUKU) three and four are required to implement sustainable finance starting in 2019, followed by BUKU one and two in 2020. Considering the study tested a sample of listed public bank sub-sectors on the Indonesia Stock Exchange (IDX) and the implementation was carried out simultaneously in 2020, the study chose the 2020–2021 period for observation. In accordance with the research gap described above, the study contributes to the literature on sustainability, by expanding the slack resources theory on green banking context when a new regulation is stipulated. The research question to be answered is: do banks use financial and potential slack effectively to conduct green activities which are then reflected in the disclosures? This question will be answered by first reviewing the related literature in the next section, followed by the research method. The analysis and interpretation of the results are then presented before the conclusion section.

2. LITERATURE REVIEW AND HYPOTHESIS DEVELOPMENT

A number of studies mostly look at the extent to which the implementation of green banking in Bangladesh affects financial performance and find that there is a positive relationship between the two (Hossain et al., 2020), which is driven by cost efficiency (Bose et al., 2021). This is also supported by Hossain and Binte Wed (2015) who examine the prevalence of the practice of green banking disclosure (GBD) and find the level of disclosure in accordance with the green banking policy. More specifically, still in the sample of banks in Bangladesh, Bose et al. (2018) prove that corporate governance mechanisms (board size and institutional ownership) positively affect the level of GBD. However, on the other hand, Julia and Kassim (2020) found that none of the sample banks met all the requirements of each green/sustainable policy. Most banks recognize the need for separate guidelines issued by the central bank for environmental initiatives and disclosure (Miah et al., 2021).

The literature on slack resources in the field of sustainability mostly focuses on disclosure of CSR and proves that the more financial sector companies in Malaysia that have slack resources, the less they disclose information related to CSR (Darus, Mad, & Yusoff, 2014). However, these results are different from Kim et al. (2019), which proves that human resource slack has a positive effect on CSR and CSR performance (Zhang, Li, et al., 2018). More specifically, Zhang, Wei, et al. (2018) found that financial slack positively moderates the effect of top management support on firms' energy-saving behavior. On the other hand, the relationship between potential slack and environmental complexity (Godoy-Bejarano et al., 2020) indicates that recoverable and potential slack increase in the same type of environment, in line with the results (Kim et al., 2017) that potential slack has a positive effect on firm performance.

In the Indonesian context, Pusva and Herlina (2017) found that the policy of PT Bank Rakyat Indonesia (BRI) Tbk in Surabaya in implementing GBD was only limited to the use of the paperless program, so it was said that it had not officially implemented green banking. This is also supported by the statement (Safitri et al., 2019), policies that lead to green banking have not been carried out by most banks in lending. Empirically, the implementation of GBD in the Indonesian banking sector is able to strengthen the relationship between CSR and the growing concern (Dewi & Dewi, 2017).

2.1. Theoretical Perspectives

Stakeholder theory generally refers to the view that companies have a responsibility not only to have a structure and a series of processes to improve business success and accountability, but also to pay attention to stakeholder interests (Russo & Perrini, 2010). Stakeholders are one of the important factors in terms of CSR disclosure (Thijssens, Bollen, & Hassink, 2015), meaning that by engaging in CSR information disclosure, companies (banks) clearly accept the rights of stakeholders to know about certain aspects of their operations (Fernando & Lawrence, 2014). This study focuses on stakeholder theory and its role in green banking activities as measured by the disclosure which is expected to reduce information asymmetry and place various types of stakeholders at the same level.

Legitimacy theory can also explain the motivation of banks engaging in green activities by conceptualizing that a company can only continue to exist if the surrounding community feels that the company operates on a value system that should be with the community's own value system (Gray, Owen, & Adams, 2009), including the regulation that governs the community. In accordance with this statement, the level of organizational legitimacy is very important for its survival (Fernando & Lawrence, 2014). This leads to the involvement of companies in disclosing CSR aimed at retaining, gaining, and regaining their legitimacy (Raimo, Vitolla, Nicolò, & Polcini, 2021). Legitimacy theory in this study provides a more comprehensive perspective on green banking (Solikhah, 2016), where every operation carried out by a bank must be in accordance with the values, norms, and expectations of the community. The expectations are also facilitated by the latest regulation concerning green activities such as the POJK 51/2017.

On the other hand, signaling theory predicted that the management of a company (including banks) can send certain signals to shareholders and investors regarding strategic management and views on future prospects. Signals will be intentionally given by companies that have good quality to shareholders or the capital market as a whole (Harmadji, Subroto, Saraswati, & Prihatiningtias, 2018), so investors are expected to be able to assess which companies have a good governance. The implementation of signaling theory in this study indicates that disclosure of green banking and efficient use of slack resources can be a good signal, so that it will have an impact on value and performance, which in turn improves the bank's reputation (Bae, Masud, & Kim, 2018).

The most relevant theory in this area is the slack resources theory which explains slack as available resources that should be utilized, allocated, and disposed effectively and efficiently to achieve organizational goals (Shang, Zhou, Hu, & Zhang, 2022). Slack resource theory views the resource as an enabler for an organization to adjust because of internal pressures or to change following external pressures (Buchholtz, Amason, & Rutherford, 1999). It is expected that when an organization's financial performance improves, slack resources will be adequately available for the company to conduct corporate environmental and social performance such as society and community relations and innovative green practices (Waddock & Graves, 1997).

2.2. Theoretical Framework

The theoretical framework of this research is described in Fig. 4.2.

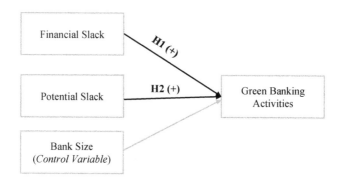

Fig. 4.2.   Research Framework.

2.3. Hypothesis Development

Financial slack is defined as available financial assets (cash on hand) that can be quickly used for various uses (Bourgeois, 1981; George, 2005). This refers to the excess that remains after the company (bank) pays various pressures from internal and external constituents, so that it is flexible and can be disbursed on managerial discretion (Mishina, Pollock, & Porac, 2004). In accordance with stakeholder theory, internal pressure comes from stakeholders who demand banks to not only focus on profits, but also protect the environment as an embodiment of the green banking concept. This is also supported by Paeleman and Vanacker (2015) that financial slack can encourage growth, because it is a flexible resource that is unused and can be allocated to unexpected growth opportunities and unpredictable problems. This statement leads to the contribution of companies in using financial slack to invest in higher fields such as CSR programs (Darus et al., 2014).

In this study, we note that bank business expansion can be done by the allocation to increase green operational responsibility, considering that if the bank is included in a financial organization with the obligation to carry out environmental tasks, so that financial slack will help finance the objectives of green banking practice. POJK Rule No. 51 of 2017 requires banks to report sustainability reports, leading to legitimacy theory, where the disclosure of green banking will imply that banks are operating in accordance with applicable norms. Previous research has shown that the existence of financial slack provides more flexibility in the implementation of CSR which is a part of green banking activities (Kim et al., 2019; Zhang et al., 2018). Based on these arguments, we develop the following hypothesis.

H1. **Financial slack has a positive effect on green banking activities.**

In addition to cash and cash equivalents (financial slack), companies (banks) need other sources of funds to finance their business, so the role of investors or creditors is very important in running a business. Companies with higher income are easier to take on additional debt so they have more potential slack (Marlin & Geiger, 2015). This is in accordance with signaling theory, that investors will invest in companies that have good signals, in this case indicated by the company's (bank) profit. Potential slack is the potential of resources obtained outside the company through debt issuance, increasing equity, or both and is defined as unused slack debt capacity (Bourgeois, 1981). The debt-to-equity ratio (DER), which is a measurement of potential slack, implies that a high DER means that the company (bank) has a relative ability to obtain funds through debt (Arora & Dharwadkar, 2011). This is also supported by the results of research (Deephouse & Wiseman, 2000), which found that companies with larger DER have lower potential slack.

In the context of this research, unused debt capacity presents a higher potential for slack or unused debt to help banks support their environmental and social tasks (in terms of green banking practice). Related research states that the higher the DER, the higher the potential slack, so that it can support environmental performance (Kim et al., 2017). However, on the other hand, Godoy-Bejarano et al. (2020) found that a lower DER represents a higher potential slack.

H2. Potential slack has a positive effect on green banking activities.

3. RESEARCH METHOD

3.1. Data and Sample

This study is a research with a quantitative approach. Data have been obtained from financial statements from Refinitiv Eikon, and sustainability reports and annual reports from the official website of the IDX. Purposive sampling is applied in obtaining the test sample in this study, where the company must include the criteria of a bank registered in IDX and disclose environmental performance in 2020–2021.

3.2. Variables

3.2.1. Dependent Variables

Green banking activities measured by the disclosure is the main dependent variable in the study, where the measurement uses a dummy variable, 1 if the bank does disclose, and 0 otherwise. The study adopted Bose et al. (2018) in calculating the variable GBDI (see Table 4.1) which contains 21 indices related to green banking practices. The total index carried out by the bank will be divided by the total indicator.

3.2.2. Independent Variables

The operationalization of the independent variables is outlined in Table 4.2.

3.2.3. Control Variable

Banks' size as the control variable is measured using the natural logarithm of total assets as described in Table 4.3.

3.3. Research Model

$$\text{GBDI} = \beta_0 + \beta_1 \text{FinSlack} + \beta_2 \text{PotSlack} + \beta_3 \text{Size} + \varepsilon$$

Note:
GBDI = Green banking disclosure index
β_0 = Constant
FinSlack = Financial slack
PotSlack = Potential slack
Size = Bank size
ε = Error

Table 4.1. Green Banking Disclosure Index.

Index	Description	Keywords
GBDI-1	Bank policy on environmental preservation and climate change	Policy, rules, regulation, environment
GBDI-2	Environmentally friendly project financing and monitoring activities	Project, environment
GBDI-3	Paperless concept or efforts to reduce paper usage/and waste processing	Paperless
GBDI-4	Adoption of policies (rules) and technology to reduce environmental disturbances in the bank's internal electronic office operations	Technology, electronic
GBDI-5	Use of environmentally friendly materials	Materials, recycle
GBDI-6	Energy conservation of business operations	Energy, solar system
GBDI-7	Efforts to reduce the impact of climate change and emissions by employees	Emission, waste
GBDI-8	Information and matters related to green product bank	Products, investment
GBDI-9	Initiatives and involvement of the bank in the construction of networks related to environmental issues	Environment, activities, organization
GBDI-10	Competently evaluate the impact of the client's previous business to impose sanctions on financing facilities	Sanctions, penalty, evaluate
GBDI-11	Organizing activities in the context of increasing environmental awareness of the people/community environment	Society, community, environment
GBDI-12	Act as an environmentally friendly bank and contribute to environmental improvement	Green, environment
GBDI-13	Awards for environmental conservation initiatives	Awards, achievement
GBDI-14	The involvement of banks in terms of supporting facilities is directly proportional to the program environment	Facilities, environment, tree
GBDI-15	Information on the establishment of a climate change fund	Climate, fund
GBDI-16	Establish a green branch to make operations more efficient	Green branch, efficiency
GBDI-17	Introduction of green marketing internally in internal communication media	Marketing, media, communication, promote
GBDI-18	Initiatives and involvement of the bank to encourage and train employees on the green movement	Training, workshop
GBDI-19	The total budget that is budgeted annually in terms of green banking practices	Budget, environment, green, estimation
GBDI-20	The actual total spent in green banking programs varies	Programs, green, environment
GBDI-21	Green banking reporting has its own separate page in the annual reports	Separate documents between sustainability and annual reports

Source: Modified from Bose et al. (2018).

Table 4.2. Measurement of Independent Variables.

No.	Slack Resource	Formulation	Source
1.	Financial slack	$FS = \dfrac{\text{firm cash} + \text{cash equivalents}}{\text{total assets}}$	Zhang, Li, et al. (2018)
2.	Potential slack	$PS = DER \left(\dfrac{\text{total liabilities}}{\text{equity}} \right)$	Arora and Dharwadkar (2011) and Marlin and Geiger (2015)

Table 4.3. Measurement of Control Variables.

No.	Control Variable	Formulation	Source
1.	Bank size	Bank size = Ln(Total Assets)	Kim et al. (2019) and Zhang, Li, et al. (2018)

4. RESULTS AND ANALYSIS

Banks listed on IDX are a test sample for the period 2020 to 2021, totaling 45 banks. However, 10 banks have not disclosed the sustainability report or annual report in 2021, so the final sample of the study is 35 banks in a 2-year period or 70 observations (refer to Table 4.4).

4.1. Descriptive Statistics

Table 4.5 describes the results of descriptive statistics on all observation variables in the research. Based on the table, the minimum GBDI value of 0.333 refers to Bank IBK Indonesia and Bank Panin Dubai Syariah in 2020, while the maximum value of 0.952 refers to Bank Rakyat Indonesia (Bank BRI) and Bank Central Asia (Bank BCA) in 2021 which have carried out environmental duties (green operations) and optimally disclosed them. The mean value of variable Y (GBDI) of 0.656 indicates that most banks have implemented the indicator of green banking practices. This also shows that they apply stakeholder theory and legitimacy theory in their companies (banks) well, supported by the statement which states that the higher the level of disclosure of information about green banking, the bank's performance in encouraging and initiating environmentally friendly project program will be even better (Bose et al., 2018). Percentage of disclosures per item is depicted in Table 4.6. The minimum effort conducted by the banks is establishing a green branch to make operations

Table 4.4. Research Sample.

Information	Number of Samples
Banks listed on IDX	45 banks
Banks that disclose sustainability reports and annual reports for 2020–2021	35 banks (1 year period)
Number of observations	*70 observations* (years 2020–2021)

Table 4.5. Descriptive Statistics.

Summarize GBDI FinSlack PotSlack Size					
Variable	Obs	Mean	Std. Dev.	Min	Max
GBDI	70	0.6564626	0.1594654	0.3333333	0.952381
FinSlack	70	0.0788437	0.0665961	0.0192795	0.3354197
PotSlack	70	5.326241	3.039951	0.4925134	17.0714
Size	70	31.61668	1.793227	28.41029	35.08436

Table 4.6. Percentage of GBDI Items for the Period 2020–2021.

Index	Description	Percentage
GBDI-1	Bank policy on environmental preservation and climate change	100
GBDI-2	Environmentally friendly project financing and monitoring activities	76
GBDI-3	Paperless concept or efforts to reduce paper usage/and waste processing	100
GBDI-4	Adoption of policies (rules) and technology to reduce environmental disturbances in the bank's internal electronic office operations	86
GBDI-5	Use of environmentally friendly materials	90
GBDI-6	Energy conservation business operations	69
GBDI-7	Efforts to reduce the impact of climate change and emissions by employees	50
GBDI-8	Information and matters related to bank green product	74
GBDI-9	Initiatives and involvement of the bank in the construction of networks related to environmental issues	79
GBDI-10	Competently evaluate the impact of the client's previous business to impose sanctions on financing facilities	76
GBDI-11	Organizing activities in the context of increasing environmental awareness of the people/community environment	88
GBDI-12	Act as an environmentally friendly bank and contribute to environmental improvement	71
GBDI-13	Awards for environmental conservation initiatives	26
GBDI-14	The involvement of banks in terms of supporting facilities is directly proportional to the program environment	88
GBDI-15	Information on the establishment of a climate change fund	40
GBDI-16	Establish a green branch to make operations more efficient	10
GBDI-17	Introduction of green marketing internally in internal communication media	31
GBDI-18	Initiatives and involvement of the bank to encourage and train employees on the green movement	50
GBDI-19	The total budget that is budgeted annually in terms of green banking practices	48
GBDI-20	The actual total spent in green banking programs varies	21
GBDI-21	Green banking reporting has its own separate page in the annual reports	48

more efficient as only 10% of the samples disclosed the existence of the branch. Indonesian banks also disclosed limited information on the actual total spent in green banking programs amid all banks have set environmental policies and paperless concept. This represents the limited information provided by banks for the green activities, programs and practices in the first two years of implementation of the POJK 51/2017 regulation.

The minimum financial slack value of 0.019 was owned by Allo Bank Indonesia, indicating that the bank only has cash and cash equivalents of Rp 89,637,176,284 to total assets, while the maximum value of 0.335 is for Bank Ina Perdana. These values and the mean (0.078) indicate that all banks have financial slack as measured by cash and cash equivalents to total assets. For the potential slack variable, the minimum value of 0.492 comes from Bank MNC International in 2021, while the maximum value of 17,071 is intended for the State Savings Bank, indicating that BTN in 2020 has a large debt capacity.

4.2. Pearson Correlations

Table 4.7 presents the correlation coefficients of the research variables. The results show that potential slack (0.3303) has a positive correlation with the GBDI, but financial slack does not show a correlation. The regression analysis below will provide a more accurate conclusion about the relationship between the two slack and GBDs. In addition, the positive correlation between GBDI and size (0.7204) implies that larger or more profitable companies tend to provide GBDs.

Table 4.8 shows the VIF of the variables less than five and the mean VIF value of 1.21 (less than ten) respectively, so that multicollinearity is not a problem in regression analysis.

4.3. Financial Slack on Green Banking Practices

Based on Table 4.9, the significance value of financial slack on the GBDI is 0.209 (more than = 0.05), implying that financial slack does not affect GBD (*H1* is rejected). This is likely because managers lack the knowledge and skills required for effective investment in social improvement (Pacheco-de-Almeida & Zemsky, 2007), given that green banking activities can lead to disproportionately higher costs. The results are also in line with Crisóstomo, de Souza Freire, and de Vasconcellos (2011), thus contradicting the slack resource theory.

4.4. Potential Slack on Green Banking Practices

The significant value of potential slack on the GBDI is 0.206 (more than = 0.05), with a negative z value of -1.26, implying that potential slack does not affect GBD (*H2* is rejected). This illustrates that banks do not use unused debt capacity to increase their environmental duties. The results are in line with Godoy-Bejarano

Table 4.7. Pearson Correlations Matrix.

	GBDI	FinSlack	PotSlack	Size
GBDI	1.0000			
FinSlack	0.1174	1.0000		
	0.3331			
PotSlack	0.3303*	0.1313	1.0000	
	0.0052	0.2785		
Size	0.7204*	0.1276	0.5213*	1.0000
	0.0000	0.2926	0.0000	

* indicates significance at 10%

Table 4.8. Variance Inflation Factor (VIF) Test.

Variable	VIF	1/ VIF
FinSlack	1.03	0.974162
PotSlack	1.40	0.716468
Size	1.39	0.719007
YEAR 2021	1.02	0.984291
Mean VIF	1.21	

Table 4.9. Regression Results Using Random Effects.

Random-effects GLS regression		Number of obs		=	70
Group variable: ID		Number of groups		=	35
R-sq:		Obs per group:			
within	= 0.1807		min =		2
between	= 0.5483		avg =		2.0
overall	= 0.5177		max =		2
		Wald chi2(3)		=	75.86
Corr(u_i, X)	= 0 (assumed)	Prob > chi2		=	0.0000

(Std. Err. adjusted for 35 clusters in ID)

GBDI	Coef.	Robust Std. Err.	z	P>|z|	[95% Conf. Interval]	
FinSlack	0.1855844	0.1477793	1.26	0.209	−0.1040577	0.4752265
PotSlack	−0.0070707	0.0055901	−1.26	0.206	−0.0180271	0.0038857
Size	0.0699548	0.0083245	8.40	0.000	0.0536391	0.0862704
_cons	−1.532247	0.2597102	−5.90	0.000	−2.04127	−1.023224
sigma_u	0.09882909					
sigma_e	0.05945128					
rho	0.73428432	(fraction of variance due to u_i)				

et al. (2020), which concluded that the high potential slack will not affect environmental performance. This may occur because the practice of green banking is one of the new tasks for banks, so that banks in Indonesia tend to use potential slack to increase profit-based bank growth rather than for green activities.

4.5. Additional Analysis

In addition to the DER, a measurement of potential slack that can describe unused debt capacity is the interest coverage ratio or ICR (Bourgeois, 1981; Bromiley, 1991), which is measured using earnings before income taxes to interest cost (Donada & Dostaler, 2005). This measurement implies that banks with higher income relative to interest costs are better able to allocate it for bank growth, such as green banking activities.

Based on the results of the Chow and Hausman tests, it is stated that the regression model is more suitable to use random effects. Table 4.10 finds that the significance of potential slack is 0.645 (exceeding = 0.05), with a negative z value of −0.46, implying that potential slack does not affect GBD, in line with the findings using DER in Table 4.9. This indicates that banks tend to prioritize ICR for profit-based activities (Ang & Straub, 1998) compared to green banking practices.

5. DISCUSSION AND CONCLUSION

This study aims to provide empirical evidence on the green activities and the association of slack resources and the environmental performance of the banking sector in Indonesia following a formal regulation on sustainable finance. The research sample consists of 35 banks listed on the IDX from 2020 to 2021, which represents the first two years of formal implementation of the regulation.

Table 4.10. Regression Results for the Additional Analysis

Random-effects GLS regression			Number of obs		=		70
Group variable: ID			Number of groups		=		35
R-sq:			Obs per group:				
within = 0.1785					min =		2
between = 0.5462					avg =		2.0
overall = 0.5138					max =		2
Corr(u_i, X) = 0 (assumed)			Wald chi2(3)		=		44.14
			Prob > chi2		=		0.0000

GBDI	Coef.	Std. Err.	z	$P>|z|$	[95% Conf. Interval]	
FinSlack	0.1586871	0.2160748	0.73	0.463	−0.2648118	0.5821859
PotSlack	−0.0036222	0.0078561	−0.46	0.645	−0.0190199	0.0117755
Size	0.0664338	0.0108943	6.10	0.000	0.0450813	0.0877862
_cons	−1.454844	0.3419103	−4.26	0.000	−2.124976	−0.7847123
sigma_u	0.09722017					
sigma_e	0.05855713					
rho	0.73379259	(fraction of variance due to u_i)				

The results show that most banks have implemented the green banking practices as reported in the disclosure. However, the slack resources, which are shown through financial slack and potential slack, show insignificant results, implying that both slacks do not affect green activities. Only bank size as a control variable shows significant results which is in line with prior literature (Bose et al., 2018; Kim et al., 2019). The larger the bank size, the more the bank will tend to optimize its growth, including in non-profit-based operations, to prove that they pay attention to sustainable development.

The insignificant role of slack resources in the midst of adequate disclosures can be interpreted to mean that the actual practices might not be as adequate and beautiful as they seem in the disclosure. In the first two years (2020–2021) of formal implementation of POJK 51/2017 regulation, most banks might prioritize the use of slack resources in handling the adverse impact of COVID-19 rather than allocating the resources to green activities. The future trends after 2021 or after the world are free from COVID-19 can be investigated further by future research. If the trend continues, then the authority needs to revisit or strengthen the regulation to increase the implementation of sustainable finance in Indonesian banking industry.

This study only uses financial slack and potential slack to describe the independent variables, while there are many slack resources that must be owned by the company. Further researchers can add to the effect of managerial slack (Zhang, Wei, et al., 2018) on green banking information disclosed by companies.

This study also uses the GBDI from Bose et al. (2018) as indicators or proxies for measuring green banking. This measurement has several limitations as it only tests the presence or absence of green banking indicators in the sample and has not seen the quality of disclosure. Future research can use a more precise and reliable measurement of environmental disclosure in the banking sector.

REFERENCES

Ang, S., & Straub, D. W. (1998). Production and transaction economies and IS outsourcing: A study of the US banking industry. *MIS Quarterly, 22*(4), 535–552.

Arora, P., & Dharwadkar, R. (2011). Corporate governance and corporate social responsibility (CSR): The moderating roles of attainment discrepancy and organization slack. *Corporate Governance: An International Review, 19*(2), 136–152. https://doi.org/10.1111/j.1467-8683.2010.00843.x

Bae, S. M., Masud, M. A. K., & Kim, J. D. (2018). A cross-country investigation of corporate governance and corporate sustainability disclosure: A signaling theory perspective. *Sustainability, 10*(8), 2611. https://doi.org/10.3390/su10082611

Bose, S., Khan, H. Z., & Monem, R. M. (2021). Does green banking performance pay off? Evidence from a unique regulatory setting in Bangladesh. *Corporate Governance: An International Review, 29*(2), 162–187. https://doi.org/10.1111/corg.12349

Bose, S., Khan, H. Z., Rashid, A., & Islam, S. (2018). What drives green banking disclosure? An institutional and corporate governance perspective. *Asia Pacific Journal of Management, 35*(2), 501–527. https://doi.org/10.1007/s10490-017-9528-x

Bourgeois, L. J. (1981). On the measurement of organizational slack. *Academy of Management Review, 6*(1), 29–39.

Bromiley, P. (1991). Testing a causal model of corporate risk taking and performance. *Academy of Management Journal, 34*(1), 37–59.

Buchholtz, A. K., Amason, A. C., & Rutherford, M. A. (1999). Beyond resources: The mediating effect of top management discretion and values on corporate philanthropy. *Business & Society, 38*(2), 167–187.

Bukhari, S. A. A., Hashim, F., Amran, A. B., & Hyder, K. (2020). Green banking and Islam: Two sides of the same coin. *Journal of Islamic Marketing, 11*(4), 977–1000. https://doi.org/10.1108/JIMA-09-2018-0154

Crisóstomo, V. L., de Souza Freire, F., & de Vasconcellos, F. C. (2011). Corporate social responsibility, firm value and financial performance in Brazil. *Social Responsibility Journal, 7*(2), 295–309. https://doi.org/10.1108/17471111111141549

Darus, F., Mad, S., & Yusoff, H. (2014). The importance of ownership monitoring and firm resources on corporate social responsibility (CSR) of financial institutions. *Procedia – Social and Behavioral Sciences, 145*, 173–180. https://doi.org/10.1016/j.sbspro.2014.06.024

de Oliveira, J. A. P., & Jabbour, C. J. C. (2017). Environmental management, climate change, CSR, and governance in clusters of small firms in developing countries: Toward an integrated analytical framework. *Business and Society, 56*(1), 130–151. https://doi.org/10.1177/0007650315575470

Deephouse, D. L., & Wiseman, R. M. (2000). Comparing alternative explanations for accounting risk-return relations. *Journal of Economic Behavior & Organization, 42*(4), 463–482.

Dewi, I. G. A. A. O., & Dewi, I. G. A. A. P. (2017). Corporate social responsibility, green banking, and going concern on banking company in Indonesia stock exchange. *International Journal of Social Sciences and Humanities, 1*(3), 118–134. https://doi.org/10.21744/ijssh.v1i3.65

Donada, C., & Dostaler, I. (2005). Relational antecedents of organizational slack: An empirical study into supplier–customer relationships. *Management, 8*(2), 25–46.

Dwaikat, L. N., & Ali, K. N. (2016). Green buildings cost premium: A review of empirical evidence. *Energy and Buildings, 110*, 396–403. https://doi.org/10.1016/j.enbuild.2015.11.021

Elkinjton, J. (1988). Partnerships from cannibals with forks: The triple bottom line of 21st-century business. *Environmental Quality Management, 8*(1), 37–51.

Falcone, P. M., & Sica, E. (2019). Assessing the opportunities and challenges of green finance in Italy: An analysis of the biomass production sector. *Sustainability (Switzerland), 11*(2), 517. https://doi.org/10.3390/su11020517

Fernando, S., & Lawrence, S. (2014). A theoretical framework for CSR practices: Integrating legitimacy theory, stakeholder theory and institutional theory. *The Journal of Theoretical Accounting, 10*(1), 149–178. https://www.sciencedirect.com/science/article/pii/S0361368217300491https://www.journals.elsevier.com/accounting-organizations-and-societyViewproject

Figge, F., & Hahn, T. (2013). Value drivers of corporate eco-efficiency: Management accounting information for the efficient use of environmental resources. *Management Accounting Research, 24*(4), 387–400. https://doi.org/10.1016/j.mar.2013.06.009

Financial Services Authority. (2020). Sustainable Finance. Available at https://www.ojk.go.id/id/pages/keuangan-berkelanjutan.aspx. Accessed on 16 June 2022.

George, G. (2005). Slack resources and the performance of privately held firms. *Academy of Management Journal, 48*(4), 661–676.

Gliedt, T., Hoicka, C. E., & Jackson, N. (2018). Innovation intermediaries accelerating environmental sustainability transitions. *Journal of Cleaner Production, 174*, 1247–1261. https://doi.org/10.1016/j.jclepro.2017.11.054

Godoy-Bejarano, J. M., Ruiz-Pava, G. A., & Téllez-Falla, D. F. (2020). Environmental complexity, slack, and firm performance. *Journal of Economics and Business, 112*, 105933. https://doi.org/10.1016/j.jeconbus.2020.105933

Gray, R., Owen, D., & Adams, C. (2009). Some theories for social accounting?: A review essay and a tentative pedagogic categorisation of theorisations around social accounting. *Environmental Accounting and Management, 4*, 1–54. https://doi.org/10.1108/s1479-3598(2010)0000004005

Harmadji, D. E., Subroto, B., Saraswati, E., & Prihatiningtias, Y. W. (2018). From theory to practice of signaling theory: Sustainability reporting strategy impact on stock price crash risk with sustainability reporting quality as mediating variable. *The 2018 Conference of Organizational Innovation, 3*(10), 647–658. https://doi.org/10.18502/kss.v3i10.3411

Hossain, A., Hossain, Md. S., Rahman, Md. M., & Karim, Md. R. (2020). The effects of green banking practices on financial performance of listed banking companies in Bangladesh. *Canadian Journal of Business and Information Studies, 2*(6), 120–128. https://doi.org/10.34104/cjbis.020.01200128

Hossain, T., & Binte Rab, N. (2015). Green banking disclosure practices: An exploratory study in Bangladesh. *The Jahangirnagar Journal of Business Studies, 5*, 109–124. https://www.researchgate.net/publication/334726142

Islam, S. M. T., Ghosh, R., & Khatun, A. (2021). Slack resources, free cash flow and corporate social responsibility expenditure: Evidence from an emerging economy. *Journal of Accounting in Emerging Economies, 11*(4), 533–551. https://doi.org/10.1108/JAEE-09-2020-0248

Jones, M. J. (2010). Accounting for the environment: Towards a theoretical perspective for environmental accounting and reporting. *Accounting Forum, 34*(2), 123–138. https://doi.org/10.1016/j.accfor.2010.03.001

Julia, T., & Kassim, S. (2020). Exploring green banking performance of Islamic banks vs conventional banks in Bangladesh based on Maqasid Shariah framework. *Journal of Islamic Marketing, 11*(3), 729–744. https://doi.org/10.1108/JIMA-10-2017-0105

Kim, B. N., Lee, N. S., Wi, J. H., & Lee, J. K. (2017). The effects of slack resources on firm performance and innovation in the Korean pharmaceutical industry. *Asian Journal of Technology Innovation, 25*(3), 387–406. https://doi.org/10.1080/19761597.2018.1434007

Kim, S. I., Shin, H., Shin, H., & Park, S. (2019). Organizational slack, corporate social responsibility, sustainability, and integrated reporting: Evidence from Korea. *Sustainability (Switzerland), 11*(16), 4445. https://doi.org/10.3390/su11164445

Lavrinenko, O., Ignatjeva, S., Ohotina, A., Rybalkin, O., & Lazdans, D. (2019). The role of green economy in sustainable development (Case study: The EU states). *Entrepreneurship and Sustainability Issues, 6*(3), 1113–1126. https://doi.org/10.9770/jesi.2019.6.3(4)

Marlin, D., & Geiger, S. W. (2015). The organizational slack and performance relationship: A configurational approach. *Management Decision, 53*(10), 2339–2355. https://doi.org/10.1108/MD-03-2015-0100

Mehedi, S., & Kuddus, A. (2017). Green banking: A case study on Dutch-Bangla Bank Ltd. *Article in Academy of Accounting and Financial Studies Journal, 21*(2), 1–20. https://www.researchgate.net/publication/322919816

Miah, M. D., Rahman, S. M., & Mamoon, M. (2021). Green banking: The case of commercial banking sector in Oman. *Environment, Development and Sustainability, 23*(2), 2681–2697. https://doi.org/10.1007/s10668-020-00695-0

Mishina, Y., Pollock, T. G., & Porac, J. F. (2004). Are more resources always better for growth? Resource stickiness in market and product expansion. *Strategic Management Journal, 25*(12), 1179–1197. https://doi.org/10.1002/smj.424

Ongena, S., Peydró, J. L., & van Horen, N. (2015). Shocks abroad, pain at home? Bank-firm-level evidence on the international transmission of financial shocks. *IMF Economic Review, 63*(4), 698–750. https://doi.org/10.1057/imfer.2015.34

Pacheco-de-Almeida, G., & Zemsky, P. (2007). The timing of resource development and sustainable competitive advantage. *Management Science, 53*(4), 651–666. https://doi.org/10.1287/mnsc.1060.0684

Paeleman, I., & Vanacker, T. (2015). Less is more, or not? On the interplay between bundles of slack resources, firm performance and firm survival. *Journal of Management Studies, 52*(6), 819–848. https://doi.org/10.1111/joms.12135

Pusva, I. D., & Herlina, E. (2017). Analysis of the implementation of green banking in achieving operational cost efficiency in the banking industry. *The Indonesian Accounting Review, 7*(2), 203. https://doi.org/10.14414/tiar.v7i2.1602

Raimo, N., Vitolla, F., Nicolò, G., & Polcini, P. T. (2021). CSR disclosure as a legitimation strategy: Evidence from the football industry. *Measuring Business Excellence, 25*(4), 493–508. https://doi.org/10.1108/MBE-11-2020-0149

Russo, A., & Perrini, F. (2010). Investigating stakeholder theory and social capital: CSR in large firms and SMEs. *Journal of Business Ethics, 91*(2), 207–221. https://doi.org/10.1007/s10551-009-0079-z

Safitri, R., Hartiwiningsih, H., & Purwadi, H. (2019). The role of law on implementation of green banking in Indonesia. *Indonesian Law Journal, 7*(1), 115–138.

Shang, L., Zhou, Y., Hu, X., & Zhang, Z. (2022). How does the absorbed slack impact corporate social responsibility? Exploring the nonlinear effect and condition in China. *Asian Business & Management*, 1–21.

Solikhah, B. (2016). An overview of legitimacy theory on the influence of company size and industry sensitivity towards CSR disclosure. *International Journal of Applied Business and Economic Research (IJABER), 14*(5), 3013–3023. https://ssrn.com/abstract=2893283

Sun, H., Rabbani, M. R., Ahmad, N., Sial, M. S., Guping, C., Zia-Ud-din, M., & Fu, Q. (2020). CSR, co-creation and green consumer loyalty: Are green banking initiatives important? A moderated mediation approach from an emerging economy. *Sustainability (Switzerland), 12*(24), 1–22. https://doi.org/10.3390/su122410688

Tang, S., & Demeritt, D. (2018). Climate change and mandatory carbon reporting: Impacts on business process and performance. *Business Strategy and the Environment, 27*(4), 437–455. https://doi.org/10.1002/bse.1985

Thijssens, T., Bollen, L., & Hassink, H. (2015). Secondary stakeholder influence on CSR disclosure: An application of stakeholder salience theory. *Journal of Business Ethics, 132*(4), 873–891. https://doi.org/10.1007/s10551-015-2623-3

van Liempd, D., & Busch, J. (2013). Biodiversity reporting in Denmark. *Accounting, Auditing and Accountability Journal, 26*(5), 833–872. https://doi.org/10.1108/AAAJ:02-2013-1232

Waddock, S. A., & Graves, S. B. (1997). The corporate social performance–financial performance link. *Strategic Management Journal, 18*(4), 303–319.

Wen, H., Lee, C. C., & Zhou, F. (2021). Green credit policy, credit allocation efficiency and upgrade of energy-intensive enterprises. *Energy Economics, 94*, 105099. https://doi.org/10.1016/j.eneco.2021.105099

Whiteman, G., Walker, B., & Perego, P. (2013). Planetary boundaries: Ecological foundations for corporate sustainability. *Journal of Management Studies, 50*(2), 307–336. https://doi.org/10.1111/j.1467-6486.2012.01073.x

Worden, S. P., Drew, J., Siemion, A., Werthimer, D., DeBoer, D., Croft, S., … Wright, J. T. (2017). Breakthrough Listen—A new search for life in the universe. *Acta Astronautica, 139*, 98–101. https://doi.org/10.1016/j.actaastro.2017.06.008

Zhang, Y., Li, J., Jiang, W., Zhang, H., Hu, Y., & Liu, M. (2018). Organizational structure, slack resources and sustainable corporate socially responsible performance. *Corporate Social Responsibility and Environmental Management, 25*(6), 1099–1107. https://doi.org/10.1002/csr.1524

Zhang, Y., Wei, Y., & Zhou, G. (2018). Promoting firms' energy-saving behavior: The role of institutional pressures, top management support and financial slack. *Energy Policy, 115*, 230–238. https://doi.org/10.1016/j.enpol.2018.01.003

Zhao, L., Li, L., Song, Y., Li, C., & Wu, Y. (2018). Research on pricing and coordination strategy of a sustainable green supply chain with a capital-constrained retailer. *Complexity, 2018*, 1–12. https://doi.org/10.1155/2018/6845970

CHAPTER 5

RELATIONSHIP BETWEEN FINANCIAL MARKET FREEDOM AND ECONOMIC GROWTH: AN EMPIRICAL EVIDENCE FROM INDIA

Amlan Ghosh

ABSTRACT

The role of financial institutions and financial intermediaries in fostering economic growth (ECO) by improving the efficiency of capital accumulation, encouraging savings, and ultimately improving the productivity of the economy has been well established by the researchers. The reforms in the financial sector worldwide during the 1980s and 1990s were aimed at ushering in greater efficiency and more competitiveness.

The impact of financial market freedom (MF) on the overall development of the financial sector and thereby the growth in an economy is one of the most important considerations for policymakers over the years. This chapter aims to examine the causal relationship between financial MF and ECO in the Indian economy in the post-reform period.

Keywords: Economic growth; financial market; market freedom; financial institutions; emerging markets; India

JEL classification: O10; O160; G280; G0; O530

Contemporary Issues in Financial Economics: Evidence from Emerging Economies
Research in Finance, Volume 37, 81–96
Copyright © 2023 by Emerald Publishing Limited
All rights of reproduction in any form reserved
ISSN: 0196-3821/doi:10.1108/S0196-382120230000037005

1. INTRODUCTION

The role of financial institutions and financial intermediaries in fostering ECO by improving the efficiency of capital accumulation, encouraging savings and ultimately improving the productivity of the economy has been well established by the researchers and economic analysts in their empirical studies (e.g., Beck & Levine, 2004; Demirguc-Kunt & Levine, 1996; Kaushal & Ghosh, 2016; King & Levine, 1993; Levine & Zervos, 1998). Studies also found that liberalization strengthens financial development and contributes to higher long-run growth (Bekaert, Harvey, & Lundblad, 2005; Henry, 2000). The monetary stability is considered as catalyst in the growth rate because of the importance of stable environments for businesses to grow (Barro, 1996; Fischer, 1993).

Financial MF refers to policies that focuses on deregulating interest rates, privatizing financial institutions, and encouraging entry of foreign financial institutions and thereby improving the market competition. The opening up of domestic markets to foreign competition may lead to the establishment of foreign bank imports with an array of new financial instruments and services with better risk management techniques. All these policy changes will help improve the efficiency of financial intermediation and information asymmetry in the domestic country, contributing to higher returns on investment and thus to higher rates of ECO (Bumann, Niels, & Robert, 2013).

Financial liberalization may affect ECO in a number of ways. First, financial liberalization improves the credit allocation by banks and non-bank financial institutions to small- and medium-sized firms, thereby aiding to increase their total factor productivity growth (Levine, 2001; Park & Park, 2014). Second, foreign investments in the domestic market will boost the local equity prices which eventually reduces the cost of capital (Bekaert & Harvey, 2000; Henry, 2000), improves the stock market liquidity, accelerates productivity, and thereby fosters the ECO (Levine, 2001). Financial liberalization is similarly linked with increased domestic competition and technology transfers which lead to potential positive influence on ECO (Levine, 2006). Conversely, there are opposite views of the financial market reforms which states that financial MF would lead to more competition among financial intermediaries such as banks and thereby reduce their profit margin. Reduced profit margin may induce the banks to take more risk in allocating loans and other risky means to improve their profitability (Demirgüç-Kunt & Detragiache, 1998). Increased risky activities of bank would result in a surge in the number of banks failures and may create instability in the financial markets (Diamond & Dybvig, 1983; Hellmann, Murdock, & Stiglitz, 2000). Many researchers have shown that financial MF does not solve the problem of asymmetric information (Stiglitz, 2000) but increases the information asymmetry due to the pressure from competition (Boot, 2000), and therefore, the problem of information asymmetry always prevails in the financial market (Stiglitz & Weiss, 1981). The development of the stock market due to the liberalized policy may impede the economic development in developing countries (Singh, 1997). The literature on the relationship between financial MF and growth of the economy is inconclusive, and the relationship varies among the different stages of economic development, quality of financial institutions, and different levels of reform complementarities (Bekaert et al., 2005; Edwards, 2001; Rodrik & Subramanian, 2009; Williamson, 1993). The complementary role of financial market reforms and the growth nexus is not definite. Therefore, it requires an economy-specific study to focus on the relationship between financial MF and growth.

The reforms in the financial sector worldwide during the 1980s and 1990s were aimed at ushering in greater efficiency and more competitiveness (Delis, 2012). The impact of financial MF on the overall development of the financial sector and thereby growth in an economy is one of the most important considerations for policymakers over the years. India introduced its reforms in the financial market in the year 1991, and the core objective of the New Economic Policy was the creation of efficient financial institutions and stable markets by introducing more MF. The core concept was liberalization, globalization, and deregulation. The new shift in less government control to more market orientation led to reforms in the financial markets and removed restrictions on trade barriers in India (Bhole, 1999). Therefore, the aim of this chapter is to examine the causal relationship between financial MF (measured by an index) and ECO in the Indian economy in the post-reform period.

The rest of the chapter is organized as follows: Section 2 provides a review of the existing literature. Section 3 discusses the methodology and data set. Section 4 exhibits the empirical results, and Section 5 is the conclusion.

2. LITERATURE REVIEW

Financial development means the process of creation and improvement in the financial structure, which includes the interaction of financial institutions, financial markets, and financial services. Therefore, the financial MF would help to improve the financial development in an economy and lead to economic development.

Emphasizing the importance of financial intermediaries, Schumpeter (1911) argued that the services provided by the financial markets are crucial for economic development. While examining this relationship, Patrick (1966) determined the "demand following" and "supply leading" patterns. In the demand following view, the growth in the economy creates demand for financial services that in turn leads to financial market development. According to the supply leading view, the growth in the financial sector leads to the mobilization of financial savings toward big investors that ultimately stimulates ECO. This raises the inquiry of causality between these two broad sectors in different economies of the world. Addressing this query, Jung (1986) found that the less-developed countries (LDCs) have a more prevailing supply leading relationship. He thus emphasized the role of financial institutions toward economic development in LDCs. Similarly, Christopoulos and Tsionas (2004) found causal relationship from financial development to ECO in the long run.

Jeanneney, Sylviane, and Liang (2006) also found that the financial market development in China is responsible for the total factor productivity growth.

There is a wealth of other literature that supports the supply leading view (e.g., Beck & Levine, 2004; Cetorelli & Gambera, 2001; Demirguc-Kunt & Levine, 1996; King & Levine, 1993; Levine, 1997; 1999; Levine & Zervos, 1998; Levine et al., 2000; Rousseau & Wachtel, 1998; Sandberg, 1978; Sylla, 2003) and asserts that the creation of financial institutions intentionally or any development in them increases the supply of financial services and therefore causes ECO. Therefore, the financial market development is crucial for growth and more MF would help to improve the financial intermediation. Existing works of literature are also available to support the demand-following view, advocating that, when the growth in the real economy increases, the demand for financial services also increases, leading to an improvement in the financial market development (Ang & McKibbin, 2007; Chang, 2011).

Researchers have furthermore suggested that the relationship between financial market development and ECO depends on the level of economic development in the individual country. Liang and Reichert (2006) found that the causality between financial development and ECO changes with the change in ECO cycle. Other studies highlighted that the financial development varies from country to country depending upon their level of financial development (Cavenaile, Gengenbach, & Palm, 2014; Rioja & Valev, 2004).

There are some studies that have found bi-directional causality between financial market development and ECO in the economy (Abu-Bader & Abu-Qarn, 2008; Hassan, Sanchez, & Yu, 2011). These studies also accord with the previous works, which show mixed results on the relationship between financial market and ECO (e.g., Al-Yousif, 2002; Arestis & Demetriades, 1997; Cavenaile & Sougne, 2012; Demetriades & Khaled, 1996; Patrick, 1966).

For sustainable ECO the trade openness and financial openness are probably the most important determinants. Extensive empirical studies have been conducted on the relationship between trade and financial openness and ECO, and the results are mixed. There are few studies which found that the financial openness has had a positive impact on ECO (Bekaert et al., 2005; Garita, 2009; Kim, Lin, & Suen, 2014; Levchenko, Ranciere, & Thoenig, 2009; Ranciere, Tornell, & Westermann, 2006) while few others (Fratzscher & Bussiere, 2004; Gine & Townsend, 2004; Tswamuno, Pardee, & Wunnava, 2007) have found that financial openness has had a negative or insignificant impact on ECO. Similarly, some studies (Marelli & Signorelli, 2011; Mercan, Gocer, Bulut, & Dam, 2013; Razmi & Refaei, 2013; Sakyi, Villaverde, Maza, & Chittedi, 2012; Zakaria & Ahmed, 2013) and Bayer (2016) found that trade openness has a positive impact on ECO, while Menyah, Nazlioglu, and Wolde-Rufael (2014) and Ulasan (2015) found no significant impact on ECO.

There are some literature which studied the relationship between financial development and ECO in Indian context but such works have concentrated mostly on either banks or insurance separately or together to study their effect on ECO (e.g., Ahmed & Ansari, 1998; Angadi, 2003; Chakraborty, 2008; Demetriades & Luintel, 1996; Ghosh, 2013; Sahoo, 2013; Vadlamannati, 2008). There is only one published literature on the relationship between economic freedom and ECO in India (Pattanaik & Nayak, 2014) which studies for a panel of selected 20 states for three time periods, 2004/2005, 2006/2007, and 2009/2010. Against these views, our study investigates the causal relationship between financial MF and ECO in India by employing time series approach for the post-MF era. Using times series approach is more fruitful than cross-country or cross-states approach, because there may be differences in the results of cross-country/states analysis that may pose a challenge to understand the findings and the causality issue cannot be answered well in cross-country model (e.g., Arestis & Demetriades, 1997; Evans, 1995; Lee, Pesaran, & Smith,1997; Quah, 1993).

3. DATA AND METHODOLOGY

This study used two variables to analyze the relationship between financial MF and the ECO in India. A number of studies used economic freedom indexes among several other variables in their analysis (e.g., Chortareas, Girardone, & Ventouri, 2013; Demirguc-Kunt, Laeven, & Levine, 2004; De Haan & Sturm, 2000; Mavrakana & Psillaki, 2019). To measure the MF, we have used the open market category information of the *Index of Economic Freedom* created by the Heritage Foundation and the *Wall Street Journal* to measure the MF of India (Heritage Foundation, 2020).

Since, the financial MF refers to policies that focuses on deregulations, privatization of financial institutions, elimination of entry barriers for foreign financial institutions, trade openness and thereby improving the market competition, we have used the open market category information of the Index of Economic Freedom created by the Heritage Foundation and the *Wall Street Journal* to measure the MF of India (Heritage Foundation, 2020). The financial MF index of India was created by taking the average of four elements (*monetary freedom, trade freedom, investment freedom*, and *financial freedom*) of open market category information which measures the open MF of economy. Each of the four elements of open MFs is graded on a scale of 0 to 100. A country's overall score is derived by averaging these open MFs, with equal weight being given to each.

The gross domestic product (ECO) at constant price has been used as a measure of ECO in India. To eliminate the heteroscedasticity, the natural logarithms of gross domestic product have been used in this study.

The specified variables denoted as:

ECO = log GDP and MF = Average of monetary freedom, trade freedom, investment freedom, and financial freedom.

In this study, we first check the stationary properties of the variables since the nonstationary time series variable might give spurious results. We will use Augmented Dickey Fuller (ADF) test to verify the stationary time series variable. Nonstationary variables may be used in our model provided the series are co-integrated. Therefore, co-integration study has also been done to verify this property. We will use the Engle and Granger (1987) co-integration test. We also check the short-run dynamics of our model by using the VAR-VECM technique.

3.1. Data and Sample Period

The study will cover a period from 1995 to 2020 constrained by the availability of the index of economic freedom from 1991 to 1992 when India started its economic liberalization and introduced market-driven freedom in the trade, investment, and financial market. This chapter is expected to offer a comprehensive evidence on the underlying causal relationship between MF and growth to formulate robust economic policies by the policymakers or financial regulators in India. MF data were calculated from the published data of the *index of economic freedom* created by the Heritage Foundation and the ECO data which are measured by GDP at constant value taken from the World Bank data base and the hand book of statistics on Indian economy, RBI.

4. STATIONARITY TESTS

Standard regression with nonstationary data leads to spurious relationship with erroneous conclusion. It, therefore, becomes pertinent to study the nature of the time series data involved in our study. In our study, two data series, one index-based series and another macroeconomic series, are used which generally follow the random walk. The stationarity of both the series has been checked by the unit root test through ADF. The results of the unit root tests are very sensitive to the assumptions about the time series under test, for example, trend, intercept, or both trend and intercept. To understand the importance of the nature of the series under the unit root test, we plot them graphically at their level values and after differencing. From Figs. 5.1 and 5.2, we can see that both the time series have some trend at their levels. Considering the particular nature of trend in both the series, we have differenced the data series once and the trends have been removed which can be seen in Figs. 5.3 and 5.4. Based on these characteristics, the ADF test is performed. The results of both the tests are summarized in

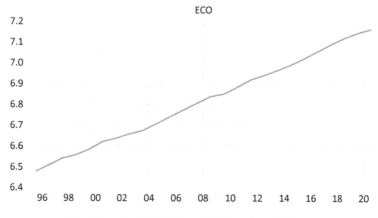

Fig. 5.1.   Graphical Plot of ECO at Level Values.

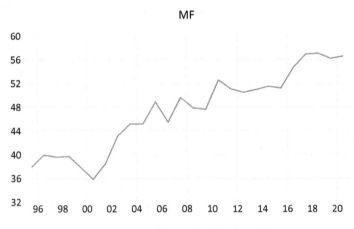

Fig. 5.2. Graphical Plot of MF at Level Values.

Table 5.1. It is clear from the ADF test (Table 5.1) that both the series (ECO and MF) have unit root at their level values at 10%, 5%, and 1% significance level. That is, the series are nonstationary. After the first differencing, the hypothesis of unit root is rejected in both series (see ADF test in Table 5.1). That is, both the series become stationary after first differencing. So, they are integrated into order one, that is, $I(1)$.

4.1. Co-integration

Co-integration tests are conducted to ascertain any long-run equilibrium relationship between these two series. The basic purpose of the co-integration test is to determine whether a group of non-stationary variables are co-integrated or

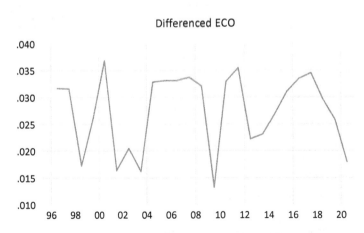

Fig. 5.3. Graphical Plot of ECO at First Difference.

Differenced MF

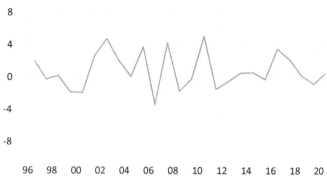

Fig. 5.4.   Graphical Plot of MF at First Difference.

not. Engle and Granger (1987) point out that the two nonstationary variables can be used in regression if the linear combination of the two nonstationary variables are stationary. In such cases, the variables are said to be co-integrated. For two series to be co-integrated, both need to be integrated in the same order. Since the two variables in our study are nonstationary and integrated of order $I(1)$, we have used the Engel–Granger co-integration test for the co-integration study. In order to test the co-integration of the series ECO and MF, we have estimated the following two equations (Equations (1) and (2)) and the residual series U_t and V_t of each estimated equation:

Table 5.1.   ADF Unit Root Test.

Variables	Null Hypothesis	ADF Test Stat.	Prob*	DW Stat	Critical Values		
					1%	5%	10%
ECO	ECO has a unit root (intercept and trend)	−2.819984	0.2041	2.021653	−4.394309	−3.612199	−3.243079
D(ECO)	ECO has a unit root (intercept)	−4.265067	0.0030	1.909092	−3.737853	−2.991878	−2.635542
MF	MF has a unit root (intercept and trend)	−3.107516	0.1262	1.905461	−4.374307	−3.603202	−3.238054
D(MF)	MF has a unit root	−5.493051	0.0000	1.997429	−2.664853	−1.955681	−1.608793

Notes: Lag Length: 1 (automatic based on modified AIC, maximum lag=4).
*MacKinnon (1996) one-sided *p*-values.

$$ECO = \alpha + \beta\,MF + U_t \tag{1}$$

$$MF = \gamma + \delta\,ECO + V_t \tag{2}$$

The results of the estimated equations are as follows:

$$ECO = 5.379948 + 0.030358\,MF$$
$$S.E\ (0.09630)\ (0.002015)$$
$$t\ (55.86283)\ (15.06846) \tag{3}$$

$$MF = -155.7495 + 29.79146\,ECO$$
$$S.E.\ (13.48512)\ (1.977074)$$
$$t\ (-11.54973)\ (15.06846) \tag{4}$$

After we obtain the residuals, we plot them graphically (Figs. 5.5 and 5.6) to see whether they contain any trend or not and then we examine the same with the help of ADF test (Table 5.2) to check the unit root property.

The ADF test on the residual series indicate that both the series are stationary at 1% level. Therefore, both the ECO and MF are co-integrated in the long run. The correlogram of the residual (unreported) series also confirms that they are stationary, that is, $I(0)$. Therefore, we can say that there is a stable long-run relationship between the ECO and MF in India.

4.2. Vector Error Correction Model (VECM)

In this model, both the series (ECO and MF) become stationary after first differencing. But differencing may result in loss of information in long-run relationship among the variables. Even if there exists a long-run equilibrium relationship

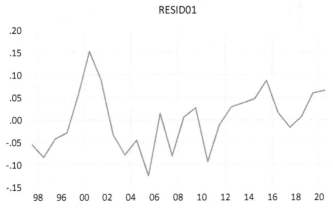

Fig. 5.5. Graphical Plot of U_t (RESID01).

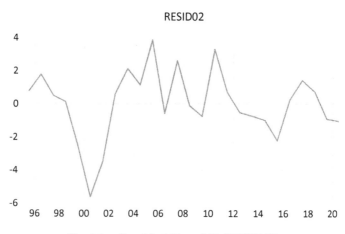

Fig. 5.6. Graphical Plot of V_t (RESID02).

between the two series, there may be disequilibrium in the short run. Engel and Granger (1987) identified that the co-integrated variables must have an error correction model (ECM) representation and a VAR model can be reformulated by means of all level variables. The vector error correction specification restricts the long-run behavior of the endogenous variables to converge to their co-integrated relationships while allowing a wide range of short-run dynamics; hence, one can treat the error terms (ET) as the "equilibrium error." Through the co-integration term, the deviation from the long-run equilibrium is corrected gradually in the course of a series of short-run adjustments.

Therefore, VECM gives us important information about the short-run relationships between these two co-integrated variables. The general form of this modified equation by employing variables of our study is presented below:

$$\Delta ECO_t = \alpha_1 + \beta_1 ET_{1t-i} + \sum_{i=1}^{n} \delta \Delta ECO_{t-i} + \sum_{i=1}^{n} \gamma \Delta MF_{t-i} + \varepsilon_t \qquad (5)$$

$$\Delta MF_t = \alpha_2 + \beta_2 ET_{2t-i} + \sum_{i=1}^{n} \theta \Delta MF_{t-i} + \sum_{i=1}^{n} \lambda \Delta ECO_{t-i} + \omega_t \qquad (6)$$

Table 5.2. ADF Unit Root Test of U_t and V_t.

Variables	Null Hypothesis	ADF Test Stat.	Prob*	DW Stat	Critical Values		
					1%	5%	10%
U_t	U_t has a unit root	−3.029518	0.0040	1.97832	−2.660720	−1.955020	−1.609070
V_t	V_t has a unit root (intercept)	−3.195084	0.0026	1.90739	−2.660720	−1.955020	−1.609070

where ε_t and ω_t are white noise ETs, and ET is equal to $ET = [\Delta ECO_{t-i} - (\Delta MF_{t-i})]$ which is the long-run effect and lagged independent variables are short-run effect. That is, changes in the dependent variables are effected by the ET, ΔECO_{t-i}, and ΔMF_{t-i}.

Before estimating the VEC model with the co-integrated vectors, it is necessary to identify and select the optimal lag length of initial VAR. Therefore, different information criteria were computed for different time lags. Based on the results of different information criteria (AIC, SIC, HQ, LR, and FPE), we have selected optimal lag 1 in our study.

4.3. Results of VECM Coefficients Estimation

The results of VECM are shown in Tables 5.3–5.5.

4.4. Findings From VECM

From VECM, the estimated equation functions have the following forms:

$$\Delta ECO_t = -0.0332 \,(ECO_{t-1} - 0.03267 \, MF_{t-1} - 5.2697)$$
$$+ 0.0130 \, \Delta ECO_{t-1} + 0.0001 \, \Delta MF_{t-1} + 0.0268 \qquad (7)$$

$$\Delta MF_t = 18.3799 \,(ECOt-1 - 0.0326 \, MF_{t-1} - 5.2697)$$
$$- 41.3319 \, \Delta ECO_{t-1} + 0.0694 \, \Delta MF_{t-1} + 1.7954 \qquad (8)$$

Table 5.3. Co-integrating Vector Coefficients.

Variables	Coefficients	"t" Statistics	Standard Errors
ECO_{t-1}	1.0000	-10.1817^*	0.0032
MF_{t-1}	-0.03267		
C	-5.269724		

Table 5.4. VECM Coefficients.

Dependent Variable	Explanatory Variable	Coefficients	"t" Statistics	Standard Errors
ΔECO_t	$ET1_{t-i}$	-0.033234	-1.20858	0.02750
	ΔECO_{t-1}	0.013007	0.05808	0.22394
	ΔMF_{t-1}	0.000147	0.17984	0.00082
	C	0.026828	4.08534	0.00657

Table 5.5. VECM Coefficients.

Dependent Variable	Explanatory Variable	Coefficients	"t" Statistics	Standard Errors
ΔMF_t	$ET2_{t-i}$	18.37997	2.36167	7.78262
	ΔECO_{t-1}	-41.33197	-0.65215	63.3781
	ΔMF_{t-1}	0.069447	0.30071	0.23094
	C	1.795410	0.96601	1.85858

From the above results, we can observe that the co-integrating vector coefficients in the long run of in both the equations are significant at 1% level. This indicates that the system is in the state of short-term dynamics. In the short run, in case of Equation (5), the dependent variable ECO_t (ECO) is significantly dependent on the first-year lagged value of the MF_t (MF) but the first-year lagged values of MF_t and ECO_t variable has no significant influence on MF_t (MF). The positive sign of ET_{2t-1} shows that the change in the value of MF_t (MF) positively depends on past errors.

4.5. The Causal Relationship

A long-run relationship suggests that there must be at least one causal relationship that exists among the ECO and the MF in India. Since both the series in our study are $I(1)$ and co-integrated, the proper statistical inference can be obtained by analyzing the causality relationship on the basis of ECM as the simple F statistic in the traditional Granger causality test does not have a standard distribution. The result of the VEC Granger causality test (Tables 5.6 and 5.7) shows that the relationship between the two variables in India is one directional which means that the MF improves the ECO in India in the post-liberalized era.

4.5.1. VEC Granger Causality
The VEC Granger causality test is shown in Tables 5.6 and 5.7.

Table 5.6. VEC Granger Causality Test: Dependent Variable: ΔECO

Dependent Variable: ΔECO			
Excluded	Chi-sq	df	Prob.
ΔMF	7.447516	1	0.0064
All	7.447516	1	0.0064

Table 5.7. VEC Granger Causality Test: Dependent Variable: ΔMF

Dependent Variable: ΔMF			
Excluded	Chi-sq	df	Prob.
ΔECO	0.269751	1	0.6035
All	0.269751	1	0.6035

5. CONCLUSION

The results of this study highlights that importance of the MF in Indian economy. The results clearly support the proposition that the MF enhances ECO in India. There is long run between the ECO and MF. In the short run, it is found that the previous year's MF has an impact on the ECO. These findings are commensurate with the findings of Bayer (2016) that trade openness have a positive impact on ECO and free trade zones efficiently increase market size which eventually leads to a more effective capital allocation thereby ECO in an economy (De Haan, Lundstrom, & Sturm, 2006; Hye & Lau, 2015; Marelli & Signorelli, 2011; Mercan et al., 2013; Romer, 1990; Sakyi et al., 2012).

The study also found that financial and monetary freedom has a positive impact on the ECO of the country and in line with the findings of Bekaert et al. (2005), Ranciere et al. (2006), Garita (2009), Levchenko et al. (2009), Kim et al. (2014), and Sarpong-Kumankoma, Abor, Aboagye, and Amidu (2018). Therefore, the reforms or more freedom in the financial market would foster the ECO in India in short run and in long run as well. Good institutional environment is the fundamental source of ECO (North, 1993). Hence, it is important for the policymakers to improve the market condition for better trade, investments and financial freedom so that business houses can trade smoothly and financial system runs efficiently with more monetary freedom to financial institutions to render improved services in the economy.

REFERENCES

Abu-Bader, S., & Abu-Qarn, A. S. (2008). Financial development and economic growth: The Egyptian experience. *Journal of Policy Modelling, 30*(5), 887–898.

Ahmed, S. M., & Ansari, M. I. (1998). Financial sector development and economic growth: The South-Asian experience. *Journal of Asian Economics, 9*(3), 503–517.

Al-Yousif, Y. K. (2002). Financial development and economic growth: Another look at the evidence from developing countries. *Review of Financial Economics, 11*(2), 131–150.

Ang, J. B., & McKibbin, W. J. (2007). Financial liberalization, financial sector development and growth: Evidence from Malaysia. *Journal of Development Economics, 84*(1), 215–233.

Angadi, V. B. (2003). Financial infrastructure and economic development: Theory, evidence and experience. *RBI Occasional Papers, 24*(1), 191–223.

Arestis, P., & Demetriades, P. (1997). Financial development and economic growth: Assessing the evidence. *The Economic Journal, 107*(442), 783–799.

Barro, R. J. (1996). *Determinants of economic growth: A cross-country empirical study*. National Bureau of Economic Research. Retrieved from http://www.nber.org/papers/w5698

Bayer, Y. (2016). Impact of openness and economic freedom on economic growth in the transition economies of the European Union. *South-Eastern Europe Journal of Economics, 1*, 7–19.

Beck, T., & Levine, R. (2004). Stock markets, banks, and growth: Panel evidence. *Journal of Banking and Finance, 28*(3), 423–442.

Bekaert, G., & Harvey, C. (2000). Foreign speculators and emerging equity markets. *Journal of Finance, 55*(2), 565–613.

Bekaert, G., Harvey, C. R., & Lundblad, C. (2005). Does financial liberalization spur growth? *Journal of Financial Economics, 77*, 3–55.

Bhole, L. M. (1999). *Financial institutions and markets: Structure, growth and innovation* (3rd ed.). New Delhi: Tata McGraw Hill.

Boot, A. W. A. (2000). Relationship banking: What do we know? *Journal of Financial Intermediation, 9*(1), 7–25.

Bumann, S., Niels, H., & Robert, L. (2013). *Journal of International Money and Finance, 33*, 255–281.

Cavenaile, L., Gengenbach, C., & Palm, F. (2014). Stock markets, banks and long run economic growth: A panel cointegration-based analysis. *De Economist, 162*(1), 19–40.

Cavenaile, L., & Sougne, D. (2012). Financial development and economic growth: An empirical investigation of the role of banks and institutional investors. *Applied Financial Economics, 22*(20), 1719–1725.

Cetorelli, N., & Gambera, M. (2001). Banking market structure, financial dependence and growth: International evidence from industry data. *The Journal of Finance, LVI*(2), 617–648.

Chakraborty, I. (2008). Does financial development cause economic growth? The case of India. *South Asia Economic Journal, 9*(1), 109–139.

Chang, H. J. (2011). Institutions and economic development: Theory, policy and history. *Journal of Institutional Economics, 7*(04), 473–498.

Chortareas, G. E., Girardone, C., & Ventouri, A. (2013). Financial freedom and bank efficiency: Evidence from the European Union. *Journal of Banking & Finance, 37*(4), 1223–1231.

Christopoulos, D. K., & Tsionas, E. G. (2004). Financial development and economic growth: Evidence from panel unit root and cointegration tests. *Journal of Development Economics, 73*(1), 55–74.

De Haan, J., & Sturm, J.-E. (2000). On the relationship between economic freedom and economic growth. *European Journal of Political Economy, 16*, 215–241.

De Haan, J., Lundstrom, S., & Sturm, J.-E. (2006). Market-oriented institutions and policies and economic growth: A critical survey. *Journal of Economic Surveys, 20*, 157–191.

Delis, M. D. (2012). Bank competition, financial reform, and institutions: The importance of being developed. *Journal of Development Economics, 97*(2), 450–465.

Demetriades, P. O., & Khaled, A. H. (1996). Does financial development cause economic growth? Time-series evidence from 16 countries. *Journal of Development Economics, 51*(2), 387–411.

Demetriades, P. O., & Luintel, K. B. (1996). Financial development, economic growth and banking sector controls: Evidence from India. *The Economic Journal, 106*(435), 359–374.

Demirgüç-Kunt, A., & Detragiache, E. (1998). *Financial liberalization and financial fragility.* IMF Working Paper 98/83, International Monetary Fund, Washington DC.

Demirguc-Kunt, A., Laeven, L., & Levine, R. (2004). Regulations, market structure, institutions, and the cost of financial intermediation. *Journal of Money, Credit and Banking, 36*(3), 593–622.

Demirguc-Kunt, A., & Levine, R. (1996). Stock markets, corporate finance, and economic growth: An overview. *The World Bank Economic Review, 10*(2), 223–239.

Diamond, D. W., & Dybvig, P. H. (1983). Bank runs, deposit insurance, and liquidity. *Journal of Political Economy, 91*(3), 410–419.

Edwards, S. (2001). *Capital mobility and economic performance: Are emerging economies different?* NBER Working Paper 8076. National Bureau of Economic Research, Inc. https://www.nber.org/system/files/working_papers/w8076/w8076.pdf.

Engle, R., & Granger, C. W. J. (1987). Co-integration and error correction: Representation, estimation and testing. *Econometrica, 55*, 251–76.

Evans, P. (1995). How to estimate growth equations consistently. Memo, Ohio State University. Presented at the 7th World Congress of the Econometric Society, Tokyo.

Fischer, S. (1993). The role of macroeconomic factors in growth. *Journal of Monetary Economics, 32*(3), 485–512.

Fratzscher, M., & Bussiere, M., (2004). *Financial openness and growth: Short-run gain, long-run pain.* ECB Working Paper No. 348. European Central Bank.

Garita, G. (2009). How does financial openness affect economic growth and its components? Retrieved from http://mpra.ub.uni-muenchen.de/20099/

Ghosh, A. (2013). Does life insurance activity promote economic development in India: An empirical analysis. *Journal of Asia Business Studies, 7*(1), 31–43.

Gine, X., & Townsend, R. M. (2004). Evaluation of financial liberalization: A general equilibrium model with constrained occupation choice. *Journal of Development Economics, 74*(2), 269–307.

Hassan, M. K., Sanchez, B., & Yu, J. S. (2011). Financial development and economic growth: New evidence from panel data. *The Quarterly Review of Economics and Finance, 51*(1), 88–104.

Hellmann, T., Murdock, K., & Stiglitz, J. E. (2000). Liberalization, moral hazard in banking and prudential regulation: Are capital requirements enough? *American Economic Review, 90*(1), 147–165.

Henry, P. B. (2000). Stock market liberalization, economic reform, and emerging market equity prices. *Journal of Finance, 55*, 529–564.

Heritage Foundation. (2020). *Index of economic freedom.* The Heritage Foundation. Retrieved from https://www.heritage.org/index/?version=684

Hye, Q. M. A., & Lau, W. Y. (2015). Trade openness and economic growth: Empirical evidence from India. *Journal of Business Economics and Management, 16*(1), 188–205.

Jeanneney, G., Sylviane, P. H., & Liang, Z. (2006). Financial development, economic efficiency, and productivity growth: Evidence from China. *The Developing Economies, 44*(1), 27–52.

Jung, W. S. (1986). Financial development and economic growth: International evidence. *Economic Development and Cultural Change, 34*(2), 333–346.

Kaushal, S., & Ghosh, A. (2016). Financial institutions and economic growth: An empirical analysis of Indian economy in the post liberalized era. *International Journal of Economics and Financial Issues, 6*(3), 1003–1013.

Kim, D. H., Lin, S. C., & Suen, Y. B. (2014). Dynamic effects of financial openness on economic growth and macroeconomic uncertainty. *Emerging Markets Finance and Trade, 48*(1), 25–54.

King, R. G., & Levine, R. (1993). Finance and growth: Schumpeter might be right. *The Quarterly Journal of Economics, 108*(3), 717–737.

Lee, K. M., Pesaran, H., & Smith, R. P. (1997). Growth and convergence in a multi-country empirical stochastic Solow model. *Journal of Applied Econometrics, 12*(4), 357–392.

Levchenko, A. A., Ranciere, R., & Thoenig, M. (2009). Growth and risk at the industry level: The real effects of financial liberalization. *Journal of Development Economics, 89*(2), 210–222.

Levine, R. (1997). Financial development and economic growth: Views and agenda. *Journal of Economic Literature, 35*(2), 688–726.

Levine, R. (1999). Law, finance, and economic growth. *Journal of Financial Intermediation, 8*(1), 8–35.

Levine, R. (2001). International financial liberalization and economic growth. *Review of International Economics, 9*(4), 688–702.

Levine, R. (2006). Finance and growth: Theory and evidence. In P. Aghion & S. Durlauf (Eds.), *Handbook of economic growth* (Vol. 1, Ch. 12, pp. 866–923). Elsevier.

Levine, R., & Zervos, S. (1998). Stock markets, banks, and economic growth. *American Economic Review, 88*(3), 537–558.

Liang, H. Y., & Reichert, A. (2006). The relationship between economic growth and banking sector development. *Banks and Bank Systems, 2*(1), 19–35.

Levine, R., Loayza, N., Beck, T. (2000), Financial intermediation and growth: Causality and causes. *Journal of Monetary Economics, 46*(1), 31–77.

MacKinnon, J. G. (1996). Numerical Distribution Functions for Unit Root and Cointegration Tests. *Journal of Applied Econometrics, 11*(6), 601–618. http://www.jstor.org/stable/2285154.

Marelli, E., & Signorelli, M. (2011). China and India: Openness, trade and effects on economic growth. *The European Journal of Comparative Economics, 8*(1), 129–154.

Mavrakana, C., & Psillaki, M. (2019). *Do economic freedom and board structure matter for bank stability and bank performance?* MPRA Paper 95709, University of Piraeus. Retrieved from https://mpra.ub.uni-muenchen.de/95709/

Menyah, K., Nazlioglu, S., & Wolde-Rufael, Y. (2014). Financial development, trade openness and economic growth in African countries: New insights from a panel causality approach. *Economic Modelling, 37*, 386–394.

Mercan, M., Gocer, I., Bulut, S., & Dam, M. (2013). The effect of openness on economic growth for BRIC-T countries: Panel data analysis. *Eurasian Journal of Business and Economics, 6*(11), 1–14.

North, D. C. (1993). *The paradox of the West*. Economics Working Paper Archive, Washington University—St. Louis, Missouri.

Park, J., & Park, Y. C. (2014). *Has financial liberalization improved economic efficiency in the Republic of Korea? Evidence from firm-level and industry-level data.* ADBI Working Paper 480, Asian Development Bank Institute. Tokyo. Retrieved from http://www.adbi.org/workingpaper/2014/05/14/6263.financial.liberalization.korea/

Patrick, H. T. (1966). Financial development and economic growth in underdeveloped countries. *Economic Development and Cultural Change, 14*(2), 174–189.

Pattanaik, F., & Nayak, N. C. (2014). Economic freedom and economic growth in India: What is the empirical relationship? *Economic Change and Restructuring, 47*, 275–298.

Quah, D. (1993). Empirical cross-section dynamics in economic growth. *European Economic Review, 37*(2), 426–434.

Ranciere, R., Tornell, A., & Westermann, F. (2006). *Decomposing the effects of financial liberalization: Crises vs. growth.* NBER Working Paper 12806. National Bureau of Economic Research, Inc. https://www.nber.org/system/files/working_papers/w12806/w12806.pdf

Razmi, M. J., & Refaei, R. (2013). The effect of trade openness and economic freedom on economic growth: The case of Middle East and East Asian countries. *International Journal of Economics and Financial Issues, 3*(2), 376–385.

Rioja, F., & Valev, N. (2004). Does one size fit all: A reexamination of the finance and growth relationship. *Journal of Development Economics, 74*(2), 429–447.

Rodrik, D., & Subramanian, A. (2009). Why did financial globalization disappoint? *IMF Staff Paper, 56*(1), 112–138.

Romer, P. M. (1990). The problem of development: A conference of the Institute for the Study of Free Enterprise Systems. *Journal of Political Economy, 98*(1), 1–11.

Rousseau, P. L., & Wachtel, P. (1998). Financial intermediation and economic performance: Historical evidence from five industrialized countries. *Journal of Money, Credit and Banking, 30*(4), 657–678.

Sahoo, S. (2013). *Financial structures and economic development in India: An empirical evaluation.* In RBI Working Paper Series No. WPS (DEPR), 02/2013. Reserve Bank of India.

Sakyi, D., Villaverde, J., Maza, A., & Chittedi, K. R. (2012). Trade openness, growth and development: Evidence from heterogeneous panel cointegration analysis for middle-income countries. *Cuadernos de Economia, 31*(57), 21–40.

Sandberg, L. G. (1978). Banking and economic growth in Sweden before World War I. *The Journal of Economic History, 38*(03), 650–680.

Sarpong-Kumankoma, E., Abor, J., Aboagye, A. Q. Q., & Amidu, M. (2018). Freedom, competition and bank profitability in Sub-Saharan Africa. *Journal of Financial Regulation and Compliance, 26*(4), 462–481.

Schumpeter, J. A. (1911). *The theory of economic development.* Cambridge, MA: Harvard University Press.

Singh, A. (1997). Financial liberalisation, stockmarkets and economic development. *The Economic Journal, 107*(442), 771–782.

Stiglitz, J. E. (2000). Capital market liberalization, economic growth, and instability. *World Development, 28*(6), 1075–1086.

Stiglitz, J. E., & Weiss, A. (1981). Credit rationing in markets with imperfect information. *American Economic Review, 71*(3), 393–410.

Sylla, R. (2003). Financial systems, risk management, and entrepreneurship: Historical perspectives. *Japan and the World Economy, 15*(4), 447–458.

Tswamuno, D. T., Pardee, S., & Wunnava, P. V. (2007). Financial liberalization and economic growth: Lessons from the South African experience. *International Journal of Applied Economics, 4*(2), 75–89.

Ulasan, B. (2015). Trade openness and economic growth: Panel evidence. *Applied Economics Letters, 22*(2), 163–167.

Vadlamannati, K. C. (2008). Do insurance sector growth and reforms affect economic development? Empirical evidence from India. *Margin: The Journal of Applied Economic Research, 2*(1), 43–86.

Williamson, J. (1993). Democracy and the 'Washington consensus'. *World Development, 21*(8), 1329–1336.

Zakaria, M., & Ahmed, E. (2013). Openness–growth nexus in Pakistan: A macro-econometric analysis. *Argumenta Oeconomica, 1*(30), 47–83.

CHAPTER 6

THE EFFECT OF eXtensible BUSINESS REPORTING LANGUAGE (XBRL) ADOPTION ON EARNINGS MANAGEMENT: EMPIRICAL EVIDENCE FROM AN EMERGING COUNTRY

Frista, Sidharta Utama and Sylvia Veronica Siregar

ABSTRACT

Purpose: *This paper aims to study the impact of adoption eXtensible Business Reporting Language (XBRL) on earnings management.*

Design/methodology/approach: *This study uses a sample of all firms listed on the Indonesian stock exchange, except for finance and real-estate sectors from 2012 to 2019, with a total of 2,560 firms–years with panel data analysis.*

Findings: *Four findings in this study are listed as follow. First, the surprising result is that accrual earnings management increase after the adoption of XBRL. Second, after the adoption of XBRL, there was an increase in real earnings management. Third, the results of the study prove that the use of Big 4 auditors will weaken the increase in real earnings management after the adoption of XBRL. Finally, this study shows that after the adoption of XBRL, it turns out that both accrual and real earnings management experienced an increase.*

Contemporary Issues in Financial Economics: Evidence from Emerging Economies
Research in Finance, Volume 37, 97–115
Copyright © 2023 by Emerald Publishing Limited
All rights of reproduction in any form reserved
ISSN: 0196-3821/doi:10.1108/S0196-382120230000037006

Originality/value: *This study contributes to providing an evaluation note to IDX regulators that the goals they want to achieve have not been achieved. This study provides empirical evidence for the debate over whether the adoption of XBRL is beneficial.*

Keywords: eXtensible Business Reporting Language; accrual earning management; real earnings management; Big 4 auditors; emerging country; agency theory

1. INTRODUCTION

eXtensible Business Reporting Language (XBRL) has become the global standard of electronic financial reporting (Bartolacci, Caputo, Fradeani, & Soverchia, 2020).

External investors will find it easier and more accurate to analyze the company's financial information compiled in XBRL format because it is easily accessible and can be compared among companies (Baldwin & Trinkle, 2011). The use of XBRL is increasingly widespread along with the belief in the benefits that will be obtained. The information taxonomy structure was developed to provide a knowledge base and insights for the XBRL taxonomy for integrated reporting (La Torre, Valentinetti, Dumay, & Rea, 2018).

Previous study provides some timely empirical evidence to the debate as to whether XBRL can improve data processing efficiency. XBRL has a nonsignificant impact on data efficiency. It suggests that the data processing efficiency benefit may have been overestimated (Rao & Guo, 2021). XBRL implementation does not have any impact on corporate tax avoidance. The results indicate that tax avoidance is not reduced following XBRL adoption (Saragih & Ali, 2022).

The obligation to submit financial reports in XBRL format has been implemented since November 2, 2015 in Indonesia. From year to year, the level of submission of financial reports in XBRL format continues to increase. For the financial reporting period, third quarter of 2019, XBRL reporting reached 95% compared to 78% in the first year of adoption. IDX continues to provide socialization and assistance for listed companies to improve their compliance with financial reporting obligations in XBRL format. The use of financial report data in XBRL format is getting wider with the IDX's plan to collaborate with several institutions related to XBRL. On January 25, 2019, IDX and the Directorate General of Taxes have signed a cooperation agreement on the utilization of data through an XBRL-based financial report submission system in the context of improving the quality of tax services. To that end, IDX will continue to develop the XBRL reporting system in order to meet the needs of industry and regulators.

Corporate governance of large corporations is complex, and subject to many laws and regulations. Recently, regulators, professional organizations, and financial reporting standard setters around the world have looked to XBRL and interactive data as a way to promote transparency of financial information and monitoring of corporate reporting. XBRL in the supply chain of business reporting contributes to transparency and monitoring, two principles of corporate governance. In the context of financial and business reporting, comprehensive corporate governance occurs at all hierarchical levels in the organization and across all divisions of responsibility, and that XBRL can help to realize a comprehensive governance system. In addition, XBRL will facilitate the delivery of corporate governance information/reports to internal and external users. It can be characterized as an end-to-end corporate governance system (Roohani, Furusho, & Koizumi, 2009).

In the context of agency theory, earnings management can be seen as agency costs. Management can perform earnings management because there is information asymmetry between management and stakeholders that allows management to manipulate the information reported to stakeholders. The adoption of XBRL can reduce the information asymmetry that exists between management and external investors (Kim, Lim, & No, 2012; Syafitri, Afdhal, & Mayapada, 2020; Tan & Shon, 2009; Yoon, Zo, & Ciganek, 2011). Information asymmetry is significantly lower in US capital markets in the XBRL era (Moore, 2019). Similar results are also observed for the capital market in Taiwan (Tzu-Yi, Fengyi, Shih-Hsuan, & Kwo-Liang, 2016). The adoption of XBRL can lead to a reduction in information asymmetry in the Korean stock market (Yoon et al., 2011).

Given the differences between accrual-based earnings management and real activities, it will be interesting to investigate the trade-offs between these two types of earnings management by corporate managers (Gao, Gao, & Wang, 2017). Adoption of an XBRL disclosure management solution (DMS) is positively associated with earnings release efficiency for companies with good news. The DMS adoption strategy is negatively related to accrual-based earnings management, but positively related to real activity-based earnings management measured by abnormal cash flows (Hsieh, Wang, & Abdolmohammadi, 2019). The surprising result is that real earnings management improved after the adoption of XBRL in China (Chen, Guo, Liu, & Tong, 2020). Real earnings management differs from accrual earnings management because real earnings management rarely violates financial regulations but real earnings management still reduces the quality of financial reporting. CEOs under pressure are more averse to taking risks to manipulate earnings through real activities after XBRL adoption (Chen et al., 2020). Thus, after the adoption of XBRL, real earnings management will increase. This study adds the effect of the moderating variable of audit quality on the relationship between the adoption of XBRL and earnings management.

The contribution of this research is as follows. This is the first study to provide evidence of the joint effect of adoption of XBRL on accrual and real earnings management. Previous studies have only provided partial evidence regarding the effects of accrual earnings management or real earnings management. This study tries to prove that after the adoption of XBRL it still occurs that both accrual and real earnings management are carried out simultaneously. As a second contribution, this study provides additional evidence for the literature related to the impact of mandatory adoption of XBRL.

2. LITERATURE REVIEW

2.1. Agency Theory

Agency theory states that the relationship between management and shareholders is seen as the relationship between agents and principals. Shareholders, as principals, delegate authority to management, as agents, to use and control the activities of the company. As a result, management has more adequate information about the company than shareholders. Information asymmetry between management and shareholders allows management to act opportunistically (Jensen & Meckling, 1976).

In the context of agency theory, earnings management can be seen as agency costs. Management can perform earnings management because there is information asymmetry between management and stakeholders that allows management to manipulate information reported to stakeholders, including income figures. Meanwhile, profit figures are one of the main considerations for stakeholders, especially investors, in assessing management performance and in making investment decisions. Therefore, earnings management can cause stakeholders to misjudge management performance and make investment decisions that can harm stakeholders (Syafitri et al., 2020). As a sophisticated information technology, XBRL helps reduce information asymmetry, and regulators are actively promoting its adoption in listed companies (Chen et al., 2020).

2.2. XBRL (eXtensible Business Reporting Language)

XBRL aims to increase accountability and transparency of business performance globally, by providing an open data exchange standard for business reporting. Often called "bar codes for reporting," XBRL makes reporting more accurate and more efficient. This allows a unique tag to be associated with the fact being reported, enabling: the person issuing the report to do so in the belief that the information contained in it can be accurately consumed and analyzed; people who consume reports to test them against a set of business and logical rules, to catch and avoid errors at source; people who use the information to do so in a way that best suits their needs, including by using a different language, alternative currency, and in their preferred style; and people who consume such information to do so believe that the data provided to them conform to a predefined set of sophisticated definitions (XBRL, 2021).

The use of XBRL is increasingly widespread along with the belief in the benefits that will be obtained. The information taxonomy structure was developed to provide a knowledge base and insights for the XBRL taxonomy for integrated reporting (La Torre et al., 2018). Many businesses, regulators, and investors can benefit from XBRL. XBRL helps integrate different business reporting procedures across business reporting jurisdictions. It reduces the costs of compliance with reporting regulations and data quality assurance services and facilitates communication between business and financial markets (Yoon et al., 2011).

2.3. Earnings Management

Earnings management occurs when managers use judgment in financial reporting and structuring transactions to alter financial statements to mislead some stakeholders about the firm's underlying economic performance, or to influence contractual outcomes that depend on reported accounting numbers (Dechow & Skinner, 2000). Studies on the determinants and consequences of earnings management are numerous, and most of these studies tend to focus on accrual-based earnings management (Dechow, Sloan, & Sweeney, 1995; Jones, 1991; Kasznik, 1999; Kothari, Leone, & Wasley, 2005).

Recently, several studies have examined the importance of earning management in real activities. Real earning management is defined as "a deviation from normal operating practices, motivated by a manager's desire to mislead at least some stakeholders into believing certain financial objectives have been met in normal operations (Roychowdhury, 2006). Typically, managers engage in real-life manipulation of activities to meet certain revenue thresholds. As such, these activities may be perceived as damaging to shareholder value. Findings from several subsequent studies imply that managers' trade accrual-based earnings management costs versus real activities. In particular, decisions about accrual-based earnings management follow real activity manipulation (Zang, 2011).

2.4. Indonesia Context

Since 2012, the IDX has started the development of reporting with XBRL. In order to carry out the reporting, the IDX must prepare a taxonomy that represents a report. As an initial development step, IDX has completed a special taxonomy for corporate financial statements. Furthermore, this taxonomy of financial statements will be disseminated to all listed companies. Reporting on the XBRL-based financial statement information is to be implemented immediately.

The reporting method based on XBRL serves to equalize the standards of different reporting formats, making it easier for users to process data. With this standard equation, issuer reporting can be used in various languages. From the aspect of monitoring the listed company, in order to be able to carry out responsive monitoring and follow-up, it is necessary to manage information that is fast, reliable, and informative for the following reasons: the increasing number of listed companies on the IDX; the increasing dynamics and complexity of corporate actions carried out by the listed company; increasing the types of reporting and disclosure of information received; and increasing types of securities and types of listed companies. From the aspect of quality of information disclosure, market and investor need for more reliable and informative information on the listed company and the barrier of language differences and differences in standards for global investors on the financial information of the listed company can be bridged by the adoption of XBRL.

The obligation to submit financial reports in XBRL format has been implemented since November 2, 2015. From year to year, the level of submission of financial reports in XBRL format continues to increase. For the third quarter of 2019 financial reporting period, XBRL reporting reached 95% compared to 78% in the first year of adoption. The IDX continues to provide socialization and assistance for listed companies to improve their compliance with financial reporting obligations in XBRL format. The use of financial report data in XBRL format is getting wider with the IDX's plan to collaborate with several institutions related to XBRL. On January 25, 2019, IDX and the Directorate General of Taxes have signed a cooperation agreement on the utilization of data through an XBRL-based financial report submission system in the context of improving the quality of tax services. To that end, IDX will continue to develop the XBRL reporting system in order to meet the needs of industry and regulators.

2.5. Hypothesis Formulation

In the context of agency theory, earnings management can be seen as agency costs. Management can perform earnings management because there is information asymmetry between management and stakeholders that allows management to manipulate information reported to stakeholders. As a sophisticated information technology, XBRL helps to reduce information asymmetry, and regulators actively promote their adoption in listed companies (Chen et al., 2020). Information asymmetry is significantly lower in US capital markets in the XBRL era (Moore, 2019).

Corporate governance of large corporations is complex and subject to many laws and regulations. Recently, regulators, professional organizations, and financial reporting standard setters around the world have looked to XBRL and interactive data as a way to promote transparency of financial information and monitor corporate reporting. XBRL in the supply chain of business reporting contributes to transparency and monitoring, two principles of corporate governance. In the context of financial and business reporting, this chapter argues that comprehensive corporate governance occurs at all hierarchical levels in the organization and across all divisions of responsibility, and that XBRL can help realize a comprehensive governance system. In addition, XBRL will facilitate the delivery of corporate governance information/reports to internal and external users. It can be characterized as an end-to-end corporate governance system (Roohani et al., 2009).

Kim et al. (2012) revealed that the amount of accrual earnings management in companies experienced a significant decrease from the period before the adoption of XBRL to the period after the adoption of XBRL explicitly. Thus, *H1a* is formulated as follows:

H1a. **After the company adopted XBRL, earnings management accruals were lower than before the adoption of XBRL.**

Adoption of an XBRL disclosure management solution (DMS) is positively associated with earnings release efficiency for companies with good news. The

DMS adoption strategy is negatively related to accrual-based earnings management, but positively related to real activity-based earnings management measured by abnormal cash flows (Hsieh et al., 2019). The surprising results of the study show that real earnings management increased after the adoption of XBRL in China (Chen et al., 2020). Real earnings management differs from accrual earnings management because it rarely violates financial regulations but still reduces the quality of financial reporting. CEOs under pressure are more averse to taking risks to manipulate earnings through real activities after XBRL adoption (Chen et al., 2020). Thus, *H1b* is formulated as follows:

H1b. After the company adopted XBRL, real earnings management was higher than before the adoption of XBRL.

Large auditors have more resources and more clients so that they do not depend on one or a few clients, in addition, because their reputation has been considered good by the community, they will audit with more caution (Craswell, 1995; Deangelo, 1981). Clients of non-Big6 auditors report discretionary accruals (DA) that increase relative earnings more than DA reported by clients of Big6 auditors (Becker, 1998).

Companies that use Big 4 auditors have better quality because they get more monitoring than companies that are not Big 4. Therefore, the use of Big 4 auditors will strengthen the effect of decreasing accrual earnings management after the adoption of XBRL. Thus, *H2a* is formulated as follows:

H2a. The use of Big 4 will strengthen the effect of the decrease in accrual earnings management after the adoption of XBRL.

As explained earlier, the companies that use Big 4 auditors have better quality, so these companies will not sacrifice their reputation by carrying out real earnings management activities. Therefore, even after the adoption of XBRL, there is a tendency to improve real earnings management. However, for companies that use Big 4 auditors, the tendency is weak to carry out real earnings management activities. Thus, *H2b* is formulated as follows (Fig. 6.1):

H2b. The use of Big 4 auditor will weaken the effect of the increase in real earnings management after the adoption of XBRL.

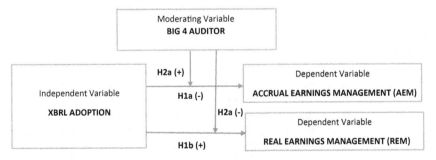

Fig. 6.1. Research framework.

3. DESIGN AND DATA

All companies listed on the IDX have been required to submit XBRL-based financial reporting since August 2015 (Indonesia Stock Exchange, 2015). The research sample consists of companies listed on the IDX in 2012–2019. The year 2020 was deliberately excluded from the sample because it had entered the beginning of the COVID-19 pandemic.

This study takes data from Refinitiv-Eikon with companies excluded from the finance and real-estate sectors. The industrial samples used include consumers, energy and utilities, healthcare, industrials, materials, and technology, as well as media and telecommunications.

The sample selection procedure is done by reducing observations with missing values from earnings management. Furthermore, it is reduced again by observations with missing control variables for the main tests, so that the total observations can be seen in Table 6.1.

3.1. Variable Measurement

3.1.1. Dependent Variable

Accrual earnings management, using DA calculated in the modified-Jones model (Dechow et al., 1995). The equations used are as follows:

$$\frac{\text{TACC}_{i,t}}{\text{TA}_{i,t-1}} = a_0 + a_1 \left(\frac{1}{\text{TA}_{i,t-1}} \right) + a_2 \left(\frac{\Delta \text{SALES}_{i,t}}{\text{TA}_{i,t-1}} \right) + a_3 \left(\frac{\text{PPE}_{i,t}}{\text{TA}_{i,t-1}} \right) + \varepsilon_{i,t}$$

where TACC is defined as earnings before extraordinary items and discontinued operations minus cash flows from operations (CFO); ΔSALES is the change in sales over the past one year; and PPE is the gross property, plant, and equipment. All variables are scaled with total assets $t-1$. DAs are computed as the residuals of the regression equation. Higher absolute values of DA are indicative of greater tendencies to engage in accruals-based earnings management.

The measures of real activities earnings management closely follow that of Hu, Kusnadi, Wang, and Wang (2020), Roychowdhury (2006), and Zang (2011). Manipulation through real operational activities is manifested through three channels: (i) *Sales manipulation*: sales manipulation can be done through providing sales discount and/or more liberal credit terms to customers in order to accelerate the recognition of sales. These strategies result in a temporary increase in sales volume, which is not sustainable in the long run once the price and credit terms revert back to normal in the near future. The real implications of engaging in these sales manipulation are that while sales revenue may be higher, the firm will realize lower CFO in the current year, as the margin from these discounted sales will be lower. Consequently, the production costs from manipulating sales are also likely to be higher. (ii) *Engaging in overproduction*: engaging in overproduction is

Table 6.1. Sample Selection Procedures.

	Industry 1	Industry 2	Industry 3	Industry 4	Industry 5	Industry 6	Number of Observation
Firm–year observations from *Refinitiv-Eikon*, between 2012 and 2019 without firms in finance and real-estate industry	1,602	522	189	1,116	720	513	4,662
Less: Observations with missing values of earnings management	(523)	(140)	(63)	(407)	(224)	(205)	(1,525)
Observations with missing control variables for the main tests	(164)	(81)	(25)	(147)	(45)	(78)	(577)
Total observations	915	301	101	562	451	230	**2,560**

Note: Industry1 is consumers; Industry2 is energy and utilities; Industry3 is healthcare; Industry4 is industrials; Industry5 materials; and Industry6 is technology, media, and telecommunication.

one way for a firm to allocate the fixed overhead costs to more units. As a result, the fixed costs and the total costs per unit produced will be lower. The cost of goods sold will also decline, and the firm can report higher earnings. However, there are additional inventory holding costs due to the additional units produced which are likely to lead to lower CFO (relative to normal production and sales level). (iii) *Reducing discretionary expenditures*: discretionary expenditures refer to expenditures on research and development, advertising, maintenance, as well as selling, general administrative (SGA). The operating costs are expensed immediately in the same year that they are incurred. Therefore, by spending less on these discretionary expenditures, a firm can manage current year earnings upwards, which may be at the expense of future earnings. The resulting effect is that the current year's CFO will be higher.

We first estimate normal level of CFO from the regression below:

$$\frac{CFO_{i,t}}{TA_{i,t-1}} = a_0 + a_1\left(\frac{1}{TA_{i,t-1}}\right) + a_2\left(\frac{SALES_{i,t}}{TA_{i,t-1}}\right) + a_3\left(\frac{\Delta SALES_{i,t}}{TA_{i,t-1}}\right) + \varepsilon_{i,t} \quad (1)$$

where TA is total assets, SALES is total sales, and ΔSALES is the change in sales over the past one year.

Meanwhile, production cost (PROD) is defined as the sum of the cost of goods sold (COGS) and (ΔSALES) is the change in inventory over the past one year; and discretionary expenses (DISCEXP) is defined as SGA expenses:

Production cost (PROD) = Cost of Goods Sold + Change in Inventory

$$\frac{COGS_{i,t}}{TA_{i,t-1}} = a_0 + a_1\left(\frac{1}{TA_{i,t-1}}\right) + a_2\left(\frac{SALES_{i,t}}{TA_{i,t-1}}\right) + \varepsilon_{i,t} \tag{2}$$

$$\frac{\Delta INV_{i,t}}{TA_{i,t-1}} = a_0 + a_1\left(\frac{1}{TA_{i,t-1}}\right) + a_2\left(\frac{SALES_{i,t}}{TA_{i,t-1}}\right) + a_3\left(\frac{\Delta SALES_{i,t}}{TA_{i,t-1}}\right) + \varepsilon_{i,t} \tag{3}$$

$$\frac{PROD_{i,t}}{TA_{i,t-1}} = a_0 + a_1\left(\frac{1}{TA_{i,t-1}}\right) + a_2\left(\frac{SALES_{i,t}}{TA_{i,t-1}}\right) + a_3\left(\frac{\Delta SALES_{i,t}}{TA_{i,t-1}}\right) + \varepsilon_{i,t} \tag{4}$$

Normal level of discretionary expenses (DISCEXP) is estimated by:

$$\frac{DISCEXP_{i,t}}{TA_{i,t-1}} = a_0 + a_1\left(\frac{1}{TA_{i,t-1}}\right) + a_2\left(\frac{SALES_{i,t-1}}{TA_{i,t-1}}\right) + \varepsilon_{i,t} \tag{5}$$

To be consistent with prior studies, we construct an aggregate measure of real activities earnings management, REM, by taking the sum of the three measures. Similarly, higher values of REM indicate that managers are more likely to engage in real activities manipulation.

3.1.2. Independent and Control Variable
Independent variable in this study using XBRL as a dummy variable equals 1 if after adopting XBRL (2015) and 0 otherwise. There are several control variables used: firm size (SIZE), defined as the natural logarithm of the total asset; leverage (LEV) is ratio of total liabilities to total assets; return on assets (ROA) is defined as earnings before extraordinary items divided by lagged total assets; loss as a dummy variable equals 1 if the firm is in loss, and 0 otherwise; market-to-book (MTB) is defined as the ratio of market value of equity to book value of equity. The use of BIG 4 auditor as a dummy variable equals 1 if the firm is audited by a Big 4 audit firm, and 0 otherwise.

3.3. Regression Models
Model (1) is used to test whether after the adoption of XBRL causes a decrease in accrual earnings management. This is used to test *H1a*.

$$DA_{i,t} = \alpha_0 + \alpha_1 XBRLi_{i,t} + \alpha_2 LEV_{i,t} + \alpha_3 SIZE_{i,t} + \alpha_4 LOSS_{i,t} + \alpha_5 ROA_{i,t} + \alpha_6 MTB_{i,t} + \epsilon_{i,t} \tag{1}$$

where for each firm, (*i*)–year; (*t*) observation; DA are the measure of accrual activities earnings management; XBRL is XBRL adoption dummy variable; LEV is the leverage ratio; SIZE is the firm size; LOSS is the company loss dummy variable; ROA is the profitability ratio; and MTB is the MTB ratio.

To test *H1b* which will test whether there is an increase in real earnings management after the adoption of XBRL, Model (2) is used.

$$REM_{i,t} = \alpha_0 + \alpha_1 XBRL_{i,t} + \alpha_2 LEV_{i,t} + \alpha_3 SIZE_{i,t} + \alpha_4 LOSS_{i,t} +$$
$$\alpha_5 ROA_{i,t} + \alpha_6 MTB_{i,t} + \epsilon_{i,t} \qquad (2)$$

where for each firm, (*i*)–year; (*t*) observation; REM is the measure of real activities earnings management and all other variables are as defined earlier.

Model (3) is used to test *H2a*, which will examine whether the use of Big 4 auditors will strengthen the decline in accrual earnings management after the adoption of XBRL.

$$DA_{i,t} = \alpha_0 + \alpha_1 XBRL_{i,t} + \alpha_2 BIG\ 4_{i,t} + \alpha_3 XBRL*BIG\ 4_{i,t} + \alpha_4 LEV_{i,t} +$$
$$\alpha_5 SIZE_{i,t} + \alpha_6 LOSS_{i,t} + \alpha_7 ROA_{i,t} + \alpha_8 MTB_{i,t} + \epsilon_{i,t} \qquad (3)$$

where for each firm, (*i*)–year; (*t*) observation; DA is the measure of accrual earnings management; XBRL is XBRL adoption dummy variable; BIG 4 is the Big 4 auditor dummy variable; XBRL*BIG 4 is an interaction variable between XBRL and Big 4 (as moderating variable); LEV is the leverage ratio; SIZE is the firm size; LOSS is the company loss dummy variable; ROA is the profitability ratio; and MTB is the market-to-book ratio.

Furthermore, Model (4) is used to test *H2b*, which will examine the moderating effect of the use of Big 4 auditor whether it will reduce the increase in real earnings management.

$$REM_{i,t} = \alpha_0 + \alpha_1 XBRL_{i,t} + \alpha_2 BIG\ 4_{i,t} + \alpha_3 XBRL*BIG\ 4_{i,t} + \alpha_4 LEV_{i,t} +$$
$$\alpha_5 SIZE_{i,t} + \alpha_6 LOSS_{i,t} + \alpha_7 ROA_{i,t} + \alpha_8 MTB_{i,t} + \epsilon_{i,t} \qquad (4)$$

where for each firm, (*i*)–year; (*t*) observation; REM is the measure of real earnings management; XBRL is XBRL adoption dummy variable; BIG 4 is the Big 4 auditor dummy variable; XBRL*BIG 4 is an interaction variable between XBRL and Big 4 (as moderating variable); LEV is the leverage ratio; SIZE is the firm size; LOSS is the company loss dummy variable; ROA is the profitability ratio; and MTB is the market-to-book ratio.

4. FINDINGS AND ANALYSIS

4.1. Descriptive Analysis

Table 6.2 reports the summary descriptive statistics for all the firm-specific variables. The sample period is from 2012 to 2019. The definition of these variables are in the Appendix.

Table 6.2. Descriptive Statistics.

Variable	N	Mean	Standard Deviation	Min	Max
DA	2,560	−0.0067512	0.1596524	−1.821158	2.520853
REM	2,560	−0.0196035	0.4058768	−6.103693	2.481982
XBRL	2,560	0.6769531	0.4677318	0.00000	1.00000
LEV	2,560	0.2855269	0.4439281	0.00000	15.74542
SIZE	2,560	28.58063	1.644373	23.1838	33.49453
LOSS	2,560	0.240625	0.4275465	0.00000	1.00000
ROA	2,560	3.774755	5.111982	−19.677	20.885
MTB	2,560	1.968368	7.026344	−201.0703	100.693

Table 6.3 reports Pearson's correlation. The sample period is from 2012 to 2019. The definition of the variables are in the Appendix. ***, **, and * indicate statistical significance at the 1%, 5%, and 10%, respectively.

4.2. Multivariate Analysis

The results contained in Table 6.4 are used to show the testing of *H1a*. Table 6.4 columns (1) and (2), which are a sample of the entire company, provide an illustration that the significant value is 0.087 (at level 10%) with a positive coefficient of 0.012 for the XBRL variable. The significant control variable SIZE has a significant value of 0.000 and a positive coefficient of 0.038. LOSS has a significant value of 0.020 and a negative coefficient of 0.025. ROA has a significant value of 0.032 and a positive coefficient of 0.002. Columns (3) and (4) in Table 6.4 are a sample for companies from the nonmanufacturing sector. The results show that the significant XBRL variable is 0.003 (at level 1%) with a coefficient of 0.039. The only significant control variable is LOSS with a significant value of 0.007 and a negative coefficient

Table 6.3. Correlation Matrices.

	DA	XBRL	LEV	SIZE	LOSS	ROA	MTB
Panel A: Accrual Earnings Management (DA)							
DA	1.0000**						
XBRL	0.0253**	1.0000**					
LEV	0.0491**	0.0127**	1.0000***				
SIZE	0.0210**	0.1237**	0.2051***	1.0000**			
LOSS	−0.0803**	0.1548**	0.2682***	−0.0433**	1.0000*		
ROA	0.0139**	−0.2102**	−0.2775***	0.0657**	−0.5419*	1.0000	
MTB	0.0346**	−0.0752**	−0.0579**	0.0687**	−0.0851*	0.1294	1.0000
	REM	XBRL	LEV	SIZE	LOSS	ROA	MTB
Panel B: Real Earnings management (REM)							
REM	1.0000**						
XBRL	0.0663**	1.0000**					
LEV	−0.0883**	0.0127**	1.0000**				
SIZE	−0.2793**	0.1237**	0.2051**	1.0000**			
LOSS	0.0629**	0.1548**	0.2682**	−0.0433**	1.0000**		
ROA	−0.0571**	−0.2102**	−0.2775**	0.0657**	−0.5419**	1.0000**	
MTB	−0.0683**	−0.0752**	−0.0579**	0.0687**	−0.0851**	0.1294**	1.0000

Table 6.4. The Impact of Adoption of XBRL on Accrual Earnings Management (DA).

Variable	Full Sample		Nonmanufacturing Sector		Manufacturing Sector	
	Coefficient (1)	*t*-Statistic (2)	Coefficient (3)	*t*-Statistic (4)	Coefficient (5)	*t*-Statistic (6)
Intercept	−1.10134020	0.000***	0.0536482	0.496	−0.0061713	0.936
XBRL	0.0126845	0.087*	0.0298222	0.003***	0.0087803	0.224
Control variable						
LEV	0.0114903	0.289	0.0012986	0.903	0.0457539	0.036**
SIZE	0.0381722	0.000***	−0.0026427	0.344	−0.0002527	0.927
LOSS	−0.0256417	0.020**	−0.0349679	0.007***	−0.0314216	0.005***
ROA	0.0025165	0.032**	−0.0001216	0.913	−0.0004186	0.638
MTB	0.0002385	0.654	−0.0000414	0.940	0.0007471	0.354
R^2	0.0207		0.0228		0.0193	
Number of observations	2,560		1,730		830	

of 0.034. Finally, Columns (5) and (6) in Table 6.4 give the result that XBRL is not significant to DA for manufacturing company, the significant value is 0.224.

These three results indicate that *H1a* is not supported. There is not enough evidence to show that accrual earnings management accruals are lower after the adoption of XBRL. The opposite result is surprising that it turns out that after the adoption of XBRL, accrual earnings management accruals are higher, especially in nonmanufacturing sector companies.

The results contained in Table 6.5 are used to show the testing of *H1b*. Columns (1) and (2) in Table 6.5, which are a sample of the entire company, provide an illustration that the significance level is 0.048 with a positive coefficient of 0.02 for the XBRL variable. The significant control variable SIZE has a significant value of 0.000 and a negative coefficient of 0.047. ROA has a significant value of 0.024 and a positive coefficient of 0.004. Columns (3) and (4) in Table 6.5 are samples for companies from the nonmanufacturing sector. The results show that the XBRL variable is not significant (0.458). The significant control variables are SIZE with a significant value of 0.000 and a negative coefficient of 0.038 and ROA with a significance level of 0.089 and a positive coefficient of 0.004. Finally, Columns (5) and (6) in Table 6.5 give the results that XBRL is significant to DA, the significant value is 0.000 and the positive coefficient is 0.093. The significant control variables are SIZE with a significant value of 0.000 and a negative coefficient of 0.077 and ROA with a significant value of 0.023 and a positive coefficient of 0.008. These results in Table 6.5 show that *H1b* is supported. This means that after the adoption of XBRL, there is an increase in real earnings management activities, especially in manufacturing sector companies.

The results contained in Table 6.6 try to prove *H2a* and *H2b*. Columns (1) and (2) in Table 6.6 show that the XBRL variable is not significant to DA (0.509). The BIG 4 variable is significant to DA, the significant value is 0.019 and the negative coefficient is 0.030. Interaction variable XBRL*Big 4 is known to be significant

Table 6.5.   The Impact of Adoption of XBRL of Real Earnings
Management (REM).

Variable	Full Sample		Nonmanufacturing Sector		Manufacturing Sector	
	Coefficient (1)	t-Statistic (2)	Coefficient (3)	t-Statistic (4)	Coefficient (5)	t-Statistic (6)
Intercept	1.2981950	0.000***	1.0505910	0.000***	2.079185	0.000***
XBRL	0.0284526	0.048**	0.0124554	0.458	0.0937210	0.000***
Control variable						
LEV	−0.0091622	0.647	−0.0134132	0.514	−0.0211130	0.843
SIZE	−0.0473888	0.000***	−0.0382993	0.000***	−0.0770697	0.000***
LOSS	0.0125840	0.570	0.0011101	0.965	0.0449949	0.282
ROA	0.0048345	0.024**	0.0042052	0.089*	0.0086550	0.023**
MTB	0.0008485	0.415	0.0011702	0.251	0.0004765	0.872
R^2	0.0395		0.0292		0.0792	
Number of observations	2,560		1,730		830	

Table 6.6.   The Effect of Using Big 4 Auditors on Adoption XBRL.

Variable	Accrual Earnings Management (DA)		Real Earnings Management (REM)	
	Coefficient (1)	t-Statistic (2)	Coefficient (3)	t-Statistic (4)
Intercept	−0.0355617	0.688	2.0659650	0.000***
XBRL	−0.0061472	0.509	0.1427033	0.000***
BIG 4	−0.0308445	0.019**	0.0927893	0.065*
XBRL*BIG 4	0.0352737	0.011**	−0.1534702	0.008***
Control variable				
LEV	0.0421364	0.057*	−0.1019209	0.200
SIZE	0.0012126	0.707	−0.0750766	0.000***
LOSS	−0.0299844	0.007***	0.0445040	0.305
ROA	−0.0003059	0.735	−0.0001017	0.976
MTB	0.0008991	0.265	−0.0044944	0.164
R^2	0.0228		0.0292	
Number of observations	830		830	

at 0.011 (at level 5%), with a positive coefficient of 0.0352. Meanwhile, the significant control variable LEV has a significant value of 0.057 and a positive coefficient of 0.042. LOSS has a significant value of 0.007 and a negative coefficient of 0.029. These results can prove that the use of BIG 4 auditor strengthens the decline in accrual earnings management after the adoption of XBRL. Thus, *H2a* is supported.

Columns (3) and (4) in Table 6.6 show that the XBRL variable has a significant value of 0.000, with a positive coefficient of 0.1427. The BIG 4 variable is significant at value 0.065 with a positive coefficient of 0.092. The interaction variable between XBRL and BIG 4 is significant at 0.008 (at level 1%) with a negative coefficient of 0.153. Thus, *H2b* is supported. These results prove that the use of BIG 4 auditor has a moderating effect that weakens the improvement in real earnings management after the adoption of XBRL. The significant control variable SIZE has a significant value of 0.000 and a negative coefficient of 0.007.

4.3. Additional Test

In order to obtain more robust results, several additional tests were carried out. First, by using an alternative measurement of real earnings management (REM_2). Alternative measurement is done by taking the average of REM_CFO, REM_DISEXP, and REM_PROD. Second, by performing a partial regression of REM_CFO, REM_DISEXP, and REM_PROD.

The test results in table 6.7 columns (1) and (2) in Table 6.7 show that the XBRL variable has a significant value of 0.000 (at level 1%), with a positive coefficient of 0.047. The BIG 4 variable is significant at the 0.065 level with a positive coefficient of 0.03. The interaction variable between XBRL and BIG 4 is significant at 0.008 (at level 1%) with a negative coefficient of 0.051.

Next, in the partial test, by using Model (5), which uses the REM_CFO variable, the results in Table 6.7 columns (3) and (4) show that the XBRL variable has a significant value 0.031 (at level 5%), with a positive coefficient of 0.018. The BIG 4 variable is significant at value 0.025 with a positive coefficient of 0.032. The interaction variable between XBRL and BIG 4 is significant at 0.073 (at level 10%) with a negative coefficient of 0.022.

$$REM\_CFO_{i,t} = \alpha_0 + \alpha_1 XBRL_{i,t} + \alpha_2 BIG\ 4_{i,t} + \alpha_3 XBRL*BIG\ 4_{i,t} + \alpha_4 LEV_{i,t} + \alpha_5 SIZE_{i,t} + \alpha_6 LOSS_{i,t} + \alpha_7 ROA_{i,t} + \alpha_8 MTB_{i,t} + \epsilon_{i,t} \quad (5)$$

Furthermore, Model (6) which uses the REM_DISEXP variable, the results are presented in columns (5) and (6) in Table 6.7 which show that the XBRL variable has a significant value of 0.000 (at level 1%), with a positive coefficient of 0.074. The BIG 4 variable is significant at value 0.098 with a positive coefficient of 0.049. The interaction variable between XBRL and BIG 4 is significant at value 0.001 (at level 1%) with a negative coefficient of 0.075.

$$REM\_DISEXP_{i,t} = \alpha_0 + \alpha_1 XBRL_{i,t} + \alpha_2 BIG\ 4_{i,t} + \alpha_3 XBRL*BIG\ 4_{i,t} + \alpha_4 LEV_{i,t} + \alpha_5 SIZE_{i,t} + \alpha_6 LOSS_{i,t} + \alpha_7 ROA_{i,t} + \alpha_8 MTB_{i,t} + \epsilon_{i,t} \quad (6)$$

$$REM\_PROD_{i,t} = \alpha_0 + \alpha_1 XBRL_{i,t} + \alpha_2 BIG\ 4_{i,t} + \alpha_3 XBRL*BIG\ 4_{i,t} + \alpha_4 LEV_{i,t} + \alpha_5 SIZE_{i,t} + \alpha_6 LOSS_{i,t} + \alpha_7 ROA_{i,t} + \alpha_8 MTB_{i,t} + \epsilon_{i,t} \quad (7)$$

Finally, Model (7) which uses the REM_PROD variable, the results are presented in columns (7) and (8) in Table 6.7 which show that the XBRL variable has a significant value of 0.034 (at level 5%), with a positive coefficient of 0.062. Meanwhile, the BIG 4 variable and the interaction variable between XBRL and BIG 4 are not significant.

Table 6.7. Additional test.

Variable	REM_2		REM_CFO		REM_DISEXP		REM_PROD	
	(1)	(2)	(3)	(4)	(5)	(6)	(7)	(8)
	Coefficient	t-Statistic	Coefficient	t-Statistic	Coefficient	t-Statistic	Coefficient	t-Statistic
Intercept	0.6886551	0.000***	0.0282431	0.816	0.1381160	0.594	1.1820490	0.334
XBRL	0.0475678	0.000***	0.0183989	0.031**	0.0748020	0.000***	0.0602186	0.034**
BIG4	0.0309298	0.065*	0.0329999	0.025**	0.0490385	0.098*	0.1141935	0.111
XBRL*BIG4	−0.0511567	0.008***	−0.0225386	0.073*	−0.0756095	0.001***	−0.0364397	0.342
Control variables								
LEV	−0.0339736	0.200	−0.0511005	0.054*	−0.0108377	0.840	0.0750381	0.516
SIZE	−0.0250255	0.000***	−0.0022703	0.605	−0.0075766	0.418	−0.0462235	0.283
LOSS	0.0148347	0.305	0.0119491	0.274	0.0209417	0.316	0.0065609	0.855
ROA	−0.0000339	0.976	0.0069881	0.000***	0.0032554	0.316	0.0044966	0.208
MTB	−0.0014981	0.164	−0.0009929	0.198	0.0024525	0.096*	0.0011678	0.646
R^2	0.0409		0.1209		0.0337		0.0146	
Number of observations	830		830		830		830	

Additional test results have provided strong evidence that after the implementation of XBRL there was an increase in real earnings management activities. Support the results of research conducted (Chen et al., 2020) the results show that there is an increase in real earnings management after the adoption of XBRL. This study provides additional evidence that companies that use BIG 4 auditors have weaker real earnings management than non-BIG 4 companies.

5. CONCLUSION

This study tries to determine whether there is a trade-off between accrual earnings management and real earnings management after the adoption of XBRL. Regulators, professional organizations, and financial reporting standard setters around the world have looked to XBRL and interactive data as a way to promote transparency of financial information and monitoring of corporate reporting. The surprising result is that accrual earnings management increased after the adoption of XBRL in Indonesia. Second, after the adoption of XBRL, there was an increase in accrual earnings management.

Apparently, after the adoption of XBRL in Indonesia, there was no trade-off between accrual earnings management and real earnings management. This study contributes to provide an evaluation note to the IDX regulator that the goals they want to achieve have not been achieved. Both accrual earnings management and real earnings management experienced an increase after the adoption of XBRL. For good results, this study proves that the use of Big 4 auditors will weaken the increase in real earnings management after the adoption of XBRL. Although there is an increase in accrual earnings management after the adoption of XBRL, this effect is weaker in companies that use Big 4 auditors.

REFERENCES

Baldwin, A. A., & Trinkle, B. S. (2011). The impact of XBRL: A Delphi investigation. *The International Journal of Digital Accounting Research, 11*, 1–24. doi:10.4192/1577-8517-v11_1

Bartolacci, F., Caputo, A., Fradeani, A., & Soverchia, M. (2020). Twenty years of XBRL: What we know and where we are going. *Meditari Accountancy Research, 29*(5), 1113–1145. doi:10.1108/medar-04-2020-0846

Becker, C. L. (1998). The Effect of Audit Quality on Earning Management. *Contemporary Accounting Research, 15.*

Chen, S., Guo, J., Liu, Q., & Tong, X. (2020). The impact of XBRL on real earnings management: Unexpected consequences of the XBRL implementation in China. *Review of Quantitative Finance and Accounting, 56*, 479–504. doi:10.1007/s11156-020-00900-1

Craswell, A. T. (1995). Auditor brand name reputations and industry Specializations.

Deangelo, L. E. (1981). Auditor independence, 'low balling', and disclosure regulation.

Dechow, P. M., & Skinner, D. J. (2000). Earnings Management: Reconciling the Views of Accounting Academics, Practitioners, and Regulators. *Accounting Horizons, 14*, 235–250. Retrieved from http://dx.doi.org/10.2308/acch.2000.14.2.235

Dechow, P. M., Sloan, R. G., & Sweeney, A. P. (1995). Detecting Earnings Management. *The Accounting Review, 70*, 193–225.

Gao, J., Gao, B., & Wang, X. (2017). Trade-off between real activities earnings management and accrual-based manipulation-evidence from China. *Journal of International Accounting, Auditing and Taxation, 29*, 66–80. doi:10.1016/j.intaccaudtax.2017.08.001

Hsieh, T.-S., Wang, Z., & Abdolmohammadi, M. (2019). Does XBRL disclosure management solution influence earnings release efficiency and earnings management? *International Journal of Accounting & Information Management, 27*(1), 74–95. doi:10.1108/ijaim-06-2017-0079

Hu, F., Kusnadi, Y., Wang, J., & Wang, Y. (2020). Insider trading restrictions and real activities earnings management. *Journal of International Financial Markets, Institutions and Money, Volume 80.*

Jensen, M. C., & Meckling, W. H. (1976). Theory of the firm: Managerial behavior, agency costs and ownership structure. *Journal of Financial Economics, 3*(4), 305–360.

Jones, J. J. (1991). Earnings management during import relief investigations. *Journal of Accounting Research, 29*(2), 193–228.

Kasznik, R. (1999). On the association between voluntary disclosure and earnings management. *Journal of Accounting Research, 37*, 57–81.

Kim, J. W., Lim, J.-H., & No, W. G. (2012). The effect of first wave mandatory XBRL reporting across the financial information environment. *Journal of Information Systems, 26*(1), 127–153. doi:10.2308/isys-10260

Kothari, S. P., Leone, A. J., & Wasley, C. E. (2005). Performance matched discretionary accrual measures. *Journal of Accounting and Economics, 39*(1), 163–197. doi:10.1016/j.jacceco.2004.11.002

La Torre, M., Valentinetti, D., Dumay, J., & Rea, M. A. (2018). Improving corporate disclosure through XBRL. *Journal of Intellectual Capital, 19*(2), 338–366. doi:10.1108/jic-03-2016-0030

Moore, J. (2019). Information Asymmetry in the U.S. Capital Market: The Relationship between Extensible Business Reporting Language and Stock Return Volatility. *Northcentral University ProQuest Dissertations Publishing.*

Rao, Y., & Guo, K. H. (2021). Does XBRL help improve data processing efficiency? *International Journal of Accounting & Information Management, 30*(1), 47–60. doi:10.1108/ijaim-07-2021-0155

Roohani, S., Furusho, Y., & Koizumi, M. (2009). XBRL: Improving transparency and monitoring functions of corporate governance. *International Journal of Disclosure and Governance, 6*(4), 355–369. doi:10.1057/jdg.2009.17

Roychowdhury, S. (2006). Earnings management through real activities manipulation. *Journal of Accounting and Economics, 42*(3), 335–370.

Saragih, A. H., & Ali, S. (2022). The effect of XBRL adoption on corporate tax avoidance: Empirical evidence from an emerging country. *Journal of Financial Reporting and Accounting.* doi:10.1108/jfra-09-2021-0281

Syafitri, R., Afdhal, M., & Mayapada, A. G. (2020). Earnings management in the pre and post eXtensible business reporting language period in Indonesia. *The Indonesian Journal of Accounting Research, 23*(01). doi:10.33312/ijar.459

Tan, C., & Shon, J. (2009). XBRL and its financial reporting benefits: Capital market evidence. *Working Paper*, Fordham University, New York.

Tzu-Yi, F., Fengyi, L., Shih-Hsuan, C., & Kwo-Liang, C. (2016). Does XBRL adoption improve information asymmetry? Evidence from Taiwan public companies. *Journal of Global Economics, 04*(01), 1–11. doi:10.4172/2375-4389.1000172

Yoon, H., Zo, H., & Ciganek, A. P. (2011). Does XBRL adoption reduce information asymmetry? *Journal of Business Research, 64*(2), 157–163. doi:10.1016/j.jbusres.2010.01.008

Zang, A. Y. (2011). Evidence on the Trade-off between real activities manipulation and accrual-based earnings management. *The Accounting Review, 87*(2), 675–703. doi:10.2308/accr-10196

APPENDIX: VARIABLE DEFINITION

Variables	Definitions
DA	Absolute value of discretionary accruals, constructed using the modified cross-sectional Jones model (Dechow et al., 1995) that controls for industry and time effects. This is a proxy for accruals earnings management
REM_CFO	Abnormal value of cash flows from operations, obtained from estimation of cross-sectional regression of equation (1) in the main text
REM_PROD	Abnormal value of production cost, obtained from estimation of cross-sectional regression of equation (4) in the main text, multiplied by -1
ABN_DISCEXP	Abnormal value of discretionary expenses, obtained from estimation of cross-sectional regression of equation (5) in the main text
REM	Composite measure of real activities earnings management, measured as the average value of RM_CFO, RM_PROD, and RM_DISCEXP. Constructed using Roychowdhury (2006). This is a proxy for real earnings management
XBRL	A dummy variable equals 1 if the after adoption of XBRL (2015) and 0 otherwise.
XBRL*BIG 4	Interaction variable between XBRL and Big 4 (as moderating variable)
Control Variables	
LEV	Ratio of total liabilities to total assets
SIZE	Firm size, defined as the natural logarithm of the total asset
ROA	Return on assets, defined as earnings before extraordinary items divided by lagged total assets
LOSS	A dummy variable equals 1 if the firm is loss, and 0 otherwise
MTB	Market-to-book, defined as the ratio of market value of equity to book value of equity
BIG 4	A dummy variable equals 1 if the firm is audited by a Big 4 audit firm, and 0 otherwise

CHAPTER 7

THE IMPACT OF LABOR RIGHTS ON EQUITY MARKET RETURNS: A CROSS-COUNTRY ANALYSIS

Robin Lieb

ABSTRACT

There is ample evidence that financial market development leads to economic growth. If improving labor rights can be shown to positively influence equity markets, then that, in turn, will lead to economic growth. The finance literature has examined the impact of a broader metric, namely, the Economic Freedom Index, on equity returns worldwide, and the evidence is mixed. This study focuses on one dimension of economic freedom: labor rights. Specifically, the study analyzes the impact of labor rights on national equity market indexes using the Labor Rights Index developed by the Organization for Economic Co-operation and Development (OECD) and the Fraser Institute (FI). Using panel regression analysis for 49 countries (for the OECD Index) and 76 countries (for the FI Index) over the period 1985–2014, the study finds that changes in labor rights have a statistically significant positive impact on equity returns, after controlling for business-cycle effects and time-fixed effects. The study also finds significant differences in the labor–rights–equity returns relationship between developed and less developed economies.

Contemporary Issues in Financial Economics: Evidence from Emerging Economies
Research in Finance, Volume 37, 117–133
Copyright © 2023 by Emerald Publishing Limited
All rights of reproduction in any form reserved
ISSN: 0196-3821/doi:10.1108/S0196-382120230000037007

1. INTRODUCTION

While the recent phenomena of technology and globalization have led to homogenization and integration of certain factors and product markets, segmentation remains in labor markets. Multinational corporations, seeking low-cost high-return business environments, continue their quest for an ideal location for their manufacturing processes. Likewise, sophisticated institutional and retail investors seek to identify attractive locations globally for their investments. One source of variations in costs and returns is the labor market. Table 7.1 provides the FI Labor Index values for a selected set of countries between 1970 and 2014. The change in the index over the 44-year period ranges from –0.1 (Bolivia) to 4.85 (United States), confirming that there is a wide variation in the progression of the index around the globe and, while some countries exhibit improving labor rights over time, others have stagnated.

There is ample evidence that financial market development leads to economic growth (see Levine, 1997, and the studies cited within). If improving labor rights can be shown to positively influence equity markets, then that, in turn, will lead to economic growth. The finance literature has examined the impact of a broader metric, namely, the Economic Freedom Index, on equity returns worldwide and the evidence is mixed (see Smimou & Karabegovic, 2010, and the studies reviewed within). This study focuses on one dimension of economic freedom: labor rights. Specifically, the study analyzes the impact of labor rights on national equity market indexes, using the Labor Rights Index developed by the OECD as well as the index developed by the FI. Using panel regression analysis for 49 countries (for the OECD Index) and 76 countries (for the FI Index) over the period 1985–2014, the study finds that changes in labor rights have a statistically significant positive impact on equity returns, after controlling for business-cycle effects and time-fixed effects.

To better understand the effect of labor rights on an educated investor's decision to invest and on a multinational corporation's decision to invest, this chapter addresses two specific issues. First, what role do labor rights play in determining stock market returns, and second, is there a significant difference in that relationship in developed versus less developed countries?

Table 7.1.   Absolute Change in the Fraser Market Regulation Index Score Between 1970 and 2014 for Selected Countries.

Country	1970	2014	Change
Argentina	3.63	5.72	2.09
Bolivia	4.7	4.6	−0.1
Canada	7.45	8.1	0.65
Indonesia	4.22	4.65	0.43
United Kingdom	6.64	8.8	2.16
United States	4.35	9.2	4.85

Source: Fraser Institute.

The rest of the chapter is organized as follows: Section 2 reviews previous research on the general relationship between economic freedom and equity returns and the relation between equity returns and various labor rights indexes. Section 3 develops the hypotheses, while Section 4 describes the data and methodology. Section 5 presents and discusses the empirical results, while Section 6 concludes with a summary of the key findings.

2. RELATED LITERATURE

Previous research in this area of finance has primarily focused on the broad relationship between economic freedom and equity returns. At the forefront, Gwartney and Lawson (2003) first defined economic freedom by creating a comprehensive economic freedom database, combining the Economic Freedom of the World Index with survey data on legal structures in different countries. Gwartney, Holcombe, and Lawson (2004) proceeded to use this index in further research to examine the issue of cross-country differences in income levels and growth rates. The results of this study show that countries with institutions and policies more consistent with economic freedom both grow more rapidly and achieve higher income levels. Additionally, the research finds that changes in institutional quality influence the future growth of per capita GDP. In the following years, research in this area picked up. Using data from the FI and market returns based on the Morgan Stanley Capital International (MSCI) equity index, Stocker (2005) shows that there is a significant direct relationship between the percentage increase in economic freedom and observed equity rates of return. Specifically, he found that a 1.0% increase in economic freedom is associated with a 2.7% increase in equity returns. Further, his study indicates that there is an inverse relationship between the beginning levels of economic freedom and observed equity returns. Less free countries have higher equity market returns. This correlation may be explained by the third observed relationship, which is an inverse relationship between the level of beginning freedom and the percentage increase in freedom. Simply put, less economically free countries are more likely to experience a greater increase in economic freedom than countries that have already achieved higher *levels* of economic freedom.

More recent research started examining the concept of economic freedom in different parts of the world such as the Middle Eastern and North African (MENA) countries, greater Asia, and developed nations. Building on Stocker's research, Smimou and Karabegovic (2010) concluded, also using data from the FI and equity index returns, that the correlation between percent changes of economic freedom and stock returns for countries in the MENA region is positive and statistically significant. The changes in economic freedom are also positively correlated with the GDP per capita. Similar studies have been conducted by Quazi (2007), with a focus on East Asia, and Bengoa and Sanchez-Robles (2003), who focused their research around Latin America. Both studies confirm the findings of Smimou and Karabegovic (2010): economic freedom has a positive impact on stock market returns.

Gospel, Pendleton, and Vitols (2014) take a different approach by looking at the impact of new investment funds (NIF) on labor rights. The NIFs encompass private equity, hedge funds, and sovereign wealth funds, which have attracted attention because of their fast growth. One key finding that emerges from their research is that the impact depends on the financial market regulation regime as well as on the labor relations regime. Strict labor legislation and union involvement in firm management can mitigate negative effects or induce private equity to pursue different strategies. The empirical evidence does show negative employment and wage effects for the Anglophone countries, where most of the NIF activity has occurred, but is less definitive in their evidence for the continental European countries.

Some studies, instead of looking at the rule of law protecting economic freedom in a certain country, used a broader measure of laws and institution. For example, Li (2002) found that institutional improvements, measured by a number of different measures of institutions, including the FI's Economic Freedom of the World Index and changes in financial technology, are the main causes of the expansion of global equity markets in recent years. Furthermore, Lawson and Roychoudhury (2008) found that firms located in the United States with increasing economic freedom experienced higher stock market returns. More recently, Billmeier and Massa (2009) examined the role of institutions (measured by the Heritage Foundation's Index of Economic Freedom), remittances, and natural resources on stock market development in 17 emerging markets in the Middle East and Central Asia from 1995 to 2005. They found that socially responsible institutions and remittances have a positive and significant impact on stock market development. Accordingly, these recent studies indicate that institutions matter for equity market development and performance. However, the specific impact of labor rights, enforced by various institutions, which have different features, was not fully examined. Hence further insights into labor rights, which is a major aspect of economic freedom, will enhance the understanding of cross-country differences and investment potential for global equity investors.

2.1. Positive Impact

While different areas around the world have been extensively covered, the aim of this chapter is not trying to widen the scope of countries but to break away from economic freedom and focus on a narrower approach. Specifically, this study will focus on the impact of labor rights, which is a small component of most economic freedom indexes, on equity returns in different countries around the globe. No research has been done in this particular area, even though past papers imply various correlations. Barnett and Salomon (2006), for instance, found a positive relationship between social responsibility and financial performance. Social screening, preferring companies that act responsibly, can lead to an increase in financial returns, implying that socially responsible behavior of companies has a positive impact. Following the Barnett and Salomon study, Edmans et al. (2014) take a similar approach by presenting research that gives stockholders and executives an idea for what influences employee satisfaction and labor market flexibility can have on stock returns. This is done by taking a list of the "Best Companies to Work For" in 14 countries and comparing it to OECD and FI data. They found that being listed as a Best Company to Work For is associated with superior returns only in countries with high labor market flexibility. These results are consistent with the idea that the recruitment, retention, and motivational benefits of employee satisfaction are most valuable in countries in which firms face fewer constraints on hiring and firing. These benefits are lower in countries with inflexible labor markets, leading to a downward shift in the marginal benefit of expenditure on employee welfare. Moreover, Edmans, Li, and Zhang (2014) state that

> in such countries, regulations already provide a floor for worker welfare, leading to a movement down the marginal benefit curve. Both forces reduce the marginal benefit of investing in worker satisfaction, and thus being listed as a Best Company may reflect an agency problem.

The study gives invaluable insight into what the results of this paper might look like. The "Best Companies to Work For" usually provide employees with special benefits, which would have a positive impact on labor rights.

2.2. Negative Impact

While multiple studies document the positive correlation between labor rights and equity returns, past research has also shown negative effects of economic freedom and labor rights on equity returns. Studies imply that more regulation and protection can represent wasteful expenditure by management. Taylor (2004) argued that workers should be treated like any input – management's goal is to extract maximum output from them while minimizing their cost. Under this view, labor rights are an indicator that employees are overpaid or underworked, both of which reduce firm value and shareholder return. Indeed, agency problems may lead to managers tolerating insufficient effort and/or excessive pay, at shareholders' expense. Further, if labor markets are laid out to protect worker's rights, it is harder to fire people. There is evidence that higher wages could potentially have a negative impact on stock prices (Bell & Machin, 2018). Building on those findings, Chen, Kacperczyk, and Ortiz-Molina (2011) show the correlation between labor unions and cost of equity. The authors hypothesize a negative relation between unionization and operating flexibility. To test their hypothesis, they use the Mandelker and Rhee degree of operating leverage (MRDOL).[1] Since an important aspect of operating flexibility is operating leverage, one would expect that unionization should increase operating leverage. The empirical results confirm their hypothesis: unionization reduces operating flexibility, which decreases equity returns and their results indicate that unionization is positively associated with MRDOL.

2.3. Cross-country Differences

With research confirming both negative and positive correlation on a more general level, it is necessary to further investigate the issue with regard to the impact on labor rights on equity returns. Previous research confirms the intuitive notion that labor rights worldwide are rather diverse. According to the OECD,

Table 7.2. Summary Statistics of MSCI Equity Returns with Respect to the OECD Employment Protection Database and the Fraser Labor Market Regulations Index over the Respective Sample Period.

| | | *MSCI Equity Returns* | | | |
Database	Mean	Standard Deviation	Coefficient of Variation	Skewness	Kurtosis
OECD (1987–2013)	3.350	1.442	43.060	3.549	15.889
Fraser (1985–2014)	3.309	1.310	39.593	4.032	20.973
		Labor Rights Indexes			
	Mean	Standard Deviation	Coefficient of Variation	Skewness	Kurtosis
OECD (1987–2013)	2.081	0.857	41.185	−0.019	−0.209
Fraser (1985–2014)	6.257	1.443	23.065	−0.018	−0.764

Table 7.3. Correlation Between MSCI Equity Returns and the OECD Employment Protection Database and the Fraser Labor Market Regulations Index over the Respective Sample Period.

1987–2013				1985–2014		
	OECD	MSCI			Fraser	MSCI
OECD	1			Fraser	1	
MSCI	0.2445	1		MSCI	0.3211	1

an intergovernmental economic organization founded to stimulate economic progress and world trade, which has been collecting data since 1985, Canada, Ireland, the United Kingdom, and the United States consistently score high when it comes to protecting labor rights. On the other hand, countries at the bottom end of the scale vary greatly over time. Over the past 10 years, Venezuela, Turkey, Uruguay, and Panama have all shared the last position in the OECD ranking at one point in time. With developed nations and third-world countries differing to a great extent on the degree of labor rights, it is important to conduct a cross-country analysis. Table 7.2 shows the summary statistics for MSCI equity returns and labor rights scores. The OECD scores are out of 6 and Fraser scores out of 10. Table 7.3 shows the correlation between equity returns and the OECD and Fraser Indexes, which shows that a somewhat weak positive relationship exists between equity returns and labor rights.

3. HYPOTHESES DEVELOPMENT

With past research covering economic freedom extensively, it is important to build on this research and further investigate what component of economic freedom causes the positive correlation. While there are distinct similarities between past research efforts, this study significantly differs from work done by Stocker (2005) or Smimou and Karabegovic (2010) in regard to sample size. By not focusing on a specific region and by increasing the time frame, the sample size for the independent and dependent variables is increased. At the same time, the study takes a narrower approach by focusing on labor rights, a small component of economic freedom.

Hence, it can be hypothesized that changes in labor rights have no impact on equity returns (H_0). Further evidence of this negative relationship is seen in Chen et al. (2011) study which implies that unionization reduces operating flexibility, which decreases equity returns. Therefore, it is possible that labor rights negatively affect equity returns.

Alternatively, it can be hypothesized that if a country supports and enforces strict labor rights such as minimum wage laws, "paid time off" (PTO), or maternity leave, changes in labor rights could have an impact on equity returns (H_1). Generally, studies have confirmed this relationship for broader research projects on economic freedom. Due to the similarities between the studies, it is arguable that labor rights positively affect equity returns.

The second hypothesis is concerned with an increase in labor rights. Based on the existing literature, it can be hypothesized that an increase in labor rights leads to an increase in equity returns (H_1). The null hypothesis in this case would state that an increase in labor rights has no impact on equity returns (H_0).

Lastly, it is important to consider how equity returns perform based on certain country criteria. Stocker (2005) indicates that there is an inverse relationship between the beginning level of economic freedom and observed equity returns, which leads to less free countries having higher equity market returns. Countries are generally classified into three groups: developed, emerging, and frontier countries. For the purpose of this last hypothesis, due to data availability, emerging and frontier markets will be combined and referred to as less developed countries.

Developed countries include Canada, the United States, Austria, Belgium, Denmark, Finland, France, Germany, Ireland, Israel, Italy, the Netherlands, Norway, Portugal, Spain Sweden, Switzerland, the United Kingdom, Australia, Hong Kong, Japan, New Zealand, and Singapore.

Less developed countries include Brazil, Chile, Colombia, Mexico, Peru, Czech Republic, Egypt, Greece, Hungary, Poland, Qatar, Russia, Saudi Arabia, South Africa, Turkey, UAE, China, India, Indonesia, South Korea, Malaysia, Pakistan, Philippines, Taiwan, Thailand, Argentina, Jamaica, Panama, Trinidad & Tobago, Bosnia Herzegovina, Bulgaria, Croatia, Estonia, Lithuania, Kazakhstan, Romania, Serbia, Slovenia, Ukraine, Botswana, Ghana, Kenya, Mauritius, Morocco, Nigeria, Tunisia, Zimbabwe, Bahrain, Jordan, Kuwait, Lebanon, Oman, Palestine, Bangladesh, Sri Lanka, and Vietnam.

Based on Stocker's assumption, it can be hypothesized that the impact of labor rights on equity returns is greater for less developed countries (H_1). The null hypothesis in this case states that the impact of labor rights on equity returns is not influenced by the developmental level countries (H_0).

4. DATA AND METHODOLOGY

4.1. Terminology

It is important to define certain terms that will be used throughout this analysis. While there is no internationally accepted definition of labor rights, Davies (2004) defines them as "entitlements that relate specifically to the role of being a worker." That description is fairly broad and can include a right to work in a job freely chosen, a right to fair working conditions, which may encompass issues as diverse as a just wage or protection of privacy, a right to be protected from arbitrary and unjustified dismissal, a right to belong to and be represented by a trade union, as well as a right to strike. These rights are either exercised individually or with others collectively. Further, it is important to note that these rights may be based on different foundations, such as freedom, dignity, or capability.

4.2. Data Description

In order to measure the pressure that labor rights put on equity returns, it is important to consider several factors; that is, the change in labor rights over time as well as the change in equity returns over the same period of time. Labor rights are measured using two different databases. The first database is the "OECD Employment Protection Database." The OECD database covers 73 countries on a yearly basis between 1987 and 2013. Due to lack of data availability, this number decreased to 49 countries. New countries are added every year; however, if a country was added to the database late, data for the respective country are only available going forward.

The second database is the FI's "Economic Freedom of the World – 2016 Annual Report" database. This database was used for general economic freedom research projects by earlier scholars. Within the database, a "Labor Market Regulations" category is available, covering 159 countries worldwide between 1985 and 2014. Due to data availability, this number is decreased to 76. The category is being extracted for the purpose of this study.

Equity returns on a yearly basis for the various countries covered in this study are available by MSCI via Thomas Reuters DataStream. Equity returns are measured by the annual returns of stock market indexes from 1985 to 2014 for Fraser data and 1987 to 2013 for OECD data. The MSCI return indices are denominated in local currency. Due to nonuniform data availability, an unbalanced panel was used.

4.3. Methodology

In the spirit of Smimou and Karabegovic (2010), this study tests for the impact of changes in labor rights on equity returns using the model in equation 1:

$$R_t = \alpha + \beta \mathrm{LR}_t + \varepsilon_t, \tag{1}$$

where R_t denotes the dependent variable (equity returns), α denotes the constant or intercept, β denotes the coefficient on changes in labor rights, which is 0 under the null hypothesis, LR_t denotes the independent variable (labor rights), and ε_t is the random component of linear relationship. To reflect controls, the model is adjusted to show the impact of macroeconomic variables on the stock market in equation 2:

$$R_t = \alpha + \beta LR_t + \xi CTRL_t + \varepsilon_t, \qquad (2)$$

where $CTRL_t$ denotes the vector of macroeconomic controls. Lastly, to scale returns, the natural logarithm of R_t is taken. This logarithmic transformation is a monotonic transformation and taking the log of the returns results in scaling the coefficients monotonically. This results in equation 3:

$$Log(R_t) = \alpha + \beta LR_t + \xi CTRL_t + \varepsilon_t \qquad (3)$$

Including all these variables, the model determines whether changes in labor rights provide additional information not captured by the business cycle fluctuations, and if not, then the coefficient on changes in labor rights, β, should equal zero. As noted by previous literature, it is important to control for as many relevant factors as possible to obtain robust results, reflected by $CTRL_t$. Hence, this study uses various macroeconomic variables from the World Development Indicators database, published by the World Bank, as control variables. The variables include gross domestic product (GDP), gross domestic product growth, gross domestic product per capita, number of listed domestic companies, population, and population growth.[2]

Further, Stocker (2005) indicates that the macroeconomic analysis of security markets is usually completed under the assumption that stock markets reflect what is expected to happen in the economy, since the expected return of a firm and its cash flow are influenced by the aggregate state of the economic environment. Under that consideration, it is necessary to expand the control variables by adding inflation and interest rate spreads (lending rate minus deposit rate), given the available data by the World Bank, to get further insights (see Diermeier, 1990). According to scholars, it is necessary to examine the impact of labor rights on equity market returns by controlling for interest rate spreads and inflation, as these variables may have an explanatory role in determining the required return to derive the value of all investments in the marketplace (see Fama, 1991a; Miller, Jeffrey, & Mandelker, 1976; Reilly, Wright, & Johnson, 2007). Moreover, past research also shows that there is substantial evidence that macroeconomic variables related to business cycles can forecast stock market returns, making this adjustment necessary (see e.g., Chen, Roll, & Ross, 1986; Fama, 1991b; Fama & French, 1989; Keim & Stambaugh, 1986). Lastly, the data were Winsorized at the 10% level to modify extreme outliers, as the data turned out to be highly volatile and includes country-fixed effects. It should be noted that all the controls mentioned above have been used in previous studies related to similar topics and have been found to be reliable, particularly in less developed country studies.

5. EMPIRICAL RESULTS AND DISCUSSION

Initially, the model in equation 3 was run with no controls. The panel regressions found that changes in the overall level of labor rights for the OECD and Fraser Indexes covering *all countries* have a positive and statistically significant impact on equity market returns (see Table 7.4, Model 1 and Table 7.5, Model 1, respectively). Over the sample period of the OECD Index (1987–2013), a 1% increase in the level of labor rights resulted in a 3.16% increase of stock market returns, statistically significant at the 1% level (Table 7.4, Model 1). Using the Fraser Index (1985–2014), a 1% increase in labor rights resulted in a 4.16% increase in equity returns, statistically significant at the 1% level (Table 7.5, Model 1).

Several macro-variable controls were then added to the model. Once again, the panel regression results imply that the significance and the magnitude of the coefficient on the changes in labor rights do not change much for either index, implying that the changes in labor rights explain a significant proportion of the variation in stock market returns, after accounting for the influence of the business cycle variables. For instance, using the Fraser Index, after taking all control variables including GDP growth, listed companies, population growth, inflation, and interest rate spreads into account, the coefficient on the changes in labor rights decreases to 3.95%, with it still being statistically significant at the 10% level (Table 7.5, Model 10). This is similar for the OECD Index, with the coefficient declining from 3.16% to 3.03% when including the relevant controls (Table 7.4, Model 10).

This evidence is confirmed for *less developed countries* as well, even though the coefficients were smaller in magnitude, overall, and fewer macroeconomic variables were statistically significant. The results imply that, over the sample period of the OECD Index covering less developed countries, a 1% increase in the level of labor rights resulted in a 1.95% increase of stock market returns, statistically significant at the 1% level (Table 7.6, Model 1). Using the Fraser Index, a 1% increase in labor rights resulted in a 5.61% increase in equity returns, statistically significant at the 1% level (Table 7.7, Model 1).

Continuing with the less developed subsample, after including macroeconomic control variables, the coefficient for the OECD Index falls to 1.41%, significant at the 1% level, while for the Fraser Index, the coefficient decreases to 2.42%, significant at the 1% level (Table 7.6, Model 10 and Table 7.7, Model 10, respectively). Further, it is important to note that the explanatory power, as measured by the adjusted R^2, was higher in the models for less developed countries.

One of the reasons for the big difference in the models focusing on less developed countries may be the fact that the sample size was decreased due to lack of data availability and the equity returns for the countries included in this smaller sample were highly volatile. The volatility in the stock markets of less developed countries may also stem from factors not included in the initial model. Despite Winsorization, the volatile nature of the less developed returns data may still have an impact on the results.

Lastly, the impact of labor rights on equity returns in *developed countries* using both indexes was insignificant. This may be explained by the fact that developed

Table 7.4. Regression Results (OECD Labor Rights Index). Stock Market Returns and Labor Rights with and Without Set of Control Variables Using (Unbalanced) Panel Data over the Sample Period, 1987–2013.

	(1)	(2)	(3)	(4)	(5)	(6)	(7)	(8)	(9)	(10)
	Dependent Variable: Annualized Equity Market Returns									
Constant	0.0654	0.0711	0.0663	0.0614	0.1457***	0.0654	0.0988**	0.0229	0.06	0.0584
	(0.0436)	(0.0434)	(0.0436)	(0.0437)	(0.053)	(0.0436)	(0.0432)	(0.0443)	(0.0616)	(0.074)
Labor rights	3.1637***	1.9211***	3.1776***	3.4475***	2.9431***	3.1572***	2.8576***	3.1789***	3.1553***	3.03***
	(0.0983)	(0.4367)	(0.1028)	(0.2317)	(0.1334)	(0.0994)	(0.1092)	(0.0972)	(0.1430)	(0.1917)
GDP		0.1014***								
		(0.0347)								
GDP growth			−0.006							−0.0306*
			(0.013)							(0.0178)
GDP per capita				−0.0575						
				(0.0425)						
Listed companies					0.0000**					−0.0001**
					(0000)					(0.0000)
Population						0.0000				
						(0.0000)				
Population growth							0.3723***			0.1737**
							(0.0615)			(0.0882)
Inflation								0.0147***		0.0112***
								(0.0035)		(0.0043)
Interest rate spread									0.0000	0.0000
									(0.0000)	(0.0000)
Country/time FE	Yes	Yes	Yes	Yes	Yes	Yes	Yes	Yes	Yes	Yes
n	751	751	751	751	696	751	750	751	549	507
Adjusted R	0.0017	0.0116	0.0006	0.0028	0.0087	0.0006	0.0469	0.0236	0.0010	0.1321

Notes: ***, **, and * denote significance at 1%, 5%, and 10%, respectively; and standard errors are in parentheses below estimated coefficients.

Table 7.5. Regression Results (Fraser Labor Market Regulations Index). Stock Market Returns and Labor Rights with and Without Set of Control Variables Using (Unbalanced) Panel Data over the Sample Period, 1985–2014.

	(1)	(2)	(3)	(4)	(5)	(6)	(7)	(8)	(9)	(10)
	Dependent Variable: Annualized Equity Market Returns									
Constant	-0.1329	-0.1419***	-0.1480***	-0.1466***	-0.1637***	-0.1497***	-0.1460***	-0.1409***	-0.100***	-0.1312***
	(0.0282)	(0.0289)	(0.0285)	(0.0285)	(0.0315)	(0.0285)	(0.0293)	(0.0286)	(0.0320)	(0.0354)
Labor rights	4.1633***	3.8225***	4.337***	4.7048***	4.3630***	4.3238***	4.2621***	4.2220***	3.6772***	3.945***
	(0.1824)	(0.4812)	(0.1905)	(0.2826)	(0.1996)	(0.1869)	(0.186)	(0.186)	(0.211)	(0.232)
GDP		0.034								
		(0.0344)								
GDP growth			-0.0269**							-0.027*
			(0.0111)							(0.0145)
GDP per capita				-0.0904**						
				(0.043)						
Listed companies					0.0000					-0.00002
					(0.0000)					(0.00006)
Population						0.0000**				
						(0.0000)				
Population growth							0.0010			0.0723**
							(0.0264)			(0.037)
Inflation								0.0008**		-0.0295***
								(0.0003)		(0.007)
Interest rate spread									0.0461***	0.061***
									(0.0050)	(0.0063)
Country/time FE	Yes	Yes	Yes	Yes	Yes	Yes	Yes	Yes	Yes	Yes
n	1,043	1,026	1,026	1,026	920	1,026	1,025	1,026	835	765
Adjusted R	**0.0199**	**0.0238**	**0.0284**	**0.0270**	**0.0265**	**0.0283**	**0.0229**	**0.0276**	**0.1092**	**0.1364**

Notes: ***, **, and * denote significance at 1%, 5%, and 10%, respectively; and standard errors are in parentheses below estimated coefficients.

Table 7.6. Regression Results (OECD Labor Right Index for Less Developed Countries). Stock Market Returns and Labor Rights with and Without Set of Control Variables Using (Unbalanced) Panel Data over the Sample Period, 1987–2013.

	(1)	(2)	(3)	(4)	(5)	(6)	(7)	(8)	(9)	(10)
	Dependent Variable: Annualized Equity Market Returns									
Constant	0.6514***	0.6807***	0.6939***	0.5550***	0.7203***	0.7196***	0.205365	0.5596**	-0.021238	-0.642
	(0.2118)	(0.2112)	(0.2166)	(0.2083)	(0.2192)	(0.2170)	(0.2441)	(0.2214)	(0.3360)	(0.4045)
Labor rights	1.9548***	3.8073***	1.9553***	3.7473***	1.9827***	1.8579***	2.6335***	2.0742***	4.1955***	1.4121***
	(0.5285)	(1.1327)	(0.5287)	(0.7316)	(0.5442)	(0.5320)	(0.5521)	(0.5344)	(0.8734)	(1.0025)
GDP		-0.1517*								
		(0.0821)								
GDP growth			-0.0295							0.0177
			(0.0311)							(0.0511)
GDP per capita				-0.3040***						
				(0.0881)						
Listed companies					-0.0003**					-0.0001
					(0.0001)					(0.0002)
Population						0.0000				
						(0.0000)				
Population growth							0.5775***			0.46**
							(0.1687)			(0.2294)
Inflation								0.0090		0.0051
								(0.0064)		(0.0081)
Interest rate spread									-0.1501***	-0.3104***
									(0.0468)	(0.0727)
Country/time FE	Yes	Yes	Yes	Yes	Yes	Yes	Yes	Yes	Yes	Yes
n	207	207	207	207	197	207	207	207	136	126
Adjusted *R*	**0.0394**	**0.0506**	**0.0390**	**0.0879**	**0.0620**	**0.0437**	**0.0872**	**0.0437**	**0.0582**	**0.1906**

Notes: ***, **, and * denote significance at 1%, 5%, and 10%, respectively; and standard errors are in parentheses below estimated coefficients.

Table 7.7. Regression Results (Fraser Labor Market Regulations Index for Less Developed Countries). Stock Market Returns and Labor Rights with and Without Set of Control Variables Using (Unbalanced) Panel Data over the Sample Period, 1985–2014.

	(1)	(2)	(3)	(4)	(5)	(6)	(7)	(8)	(9)	(10)
	Dependent Variable: Annualized Equity Market Returns									
Constant	-0.3747***	-0.4444***	-0.4106***	-0.4278***	-0.4317***	-0.424***	-0.4408***	-0.4010***	-0.3204***	-0.4862***
	(0.0472)	(0.0507)	(0.0481)	(0.0480)	(0.0522)	(0.0483)	(0.0507)	(0.0484)	(0.0542)	(0.0633)
Labor rights	5.6143***	7.3582***	6.0178***	6.9698***	6.13***	6.0337***	5.9642***	5.8033***	4.9941***	2.4166***
	(0.29)	(0.7328)	(0.3152)	(0.4280)	(0.3336)	(0.3118)	(0.3112)	(0.3094)	(0.355)	(1.3101)
GDP		-0.1035**								
		(0.0459)								
GDP growth			-0.0333**							-0.0305
			(0.0152)							(0.0203)
GDP per capita				-0.2028***						
				(0.0548)						
Listed companies					-0.0002***					-0.0007***
					(0.0000)					(0.0002)
Population						-0.0000***				
						(0.0000)				
Population growth							0.0695**			0.1466***
							(0.0337)			(0.0476)
Inflation								0.0006		-0.0334***
								(0.0004)		(0.0085)
Interest rate spread									0.0445***	0.0556***
									(0.0060)	(0.0075)
Country/time FE	Yes	Yes	Yes	Yes	Yes	Yes	Yes	Yes	Yes	Yes
n	653	636	636	636	566	636	635	636	524	471
Adjusted R	**0.0868**	**0.1058**	**0.1053**	**0.1176**	**0.1153**	**0.1102**	**0.1046**	**0.1016**	**0.1651**	**0.2307**

Notes: ***, ** and * denote significance at 1%, 5%, and 10% respectively; and standard errors are in parentheses below estimated coefficients.

countries already have a high labor rights index and the index does not improve or vary much over the sample period, suggesting that there may be an optimal level of labor returns that economies can achieve as implied by equity index returns. Further, minor changes in labor rights that could have increased equity returns, such as the increase of an already existing minimum wage, would not have increased the advanced countries' labor rights score in either database due to the way the index is constructed by the OECD and the FI.

In sum, the empirical analysis finds that the first hypothesis is rejected suggesting that a change in labor rights does indeed have a statistically significant impact on equity returns. Further, the results imply that the second hypothesis is strongly supported as well: an increase in labor rights leads to an increase in equity returns. Lastly, the hypothesis that the impact of labor rights on equity returns is different between developed and less developed countries is supported as well with the finding that the impact is greater for less developed countries.

6. SUMMARY AND CONCLUSIONS

The purpose of this study was to conduct a cross-country analysis of the impact of labor rights on equity returns. Using a panel regression analysis for 49 countries (for the OECD Index) and 76 countries (for the FI Index) over the period 1985 through 2014, the empirical results show that changes in labor rights have a statistically significant positive impact on equity returns, with the impact being lower in magnitude but still statistically significant and positive in less developed countries.

This study, while examining one component of economic freedom, Labor Rights, contributes to the broader body of existing literature on the positive impact of economic freedom and is consistent with the evidence provided by previous research. Further, the findings in this study point to practical and policy implications that may be of interest to both federal governments and private investors. One practical implication is that investors can improve their returns if they hold stocks in countries which increased their degree of economic freedom, rather than countries that do not build on improving labor rights. This may also be relevant for institutional investors and mutual fund managers as part of their asset allocation strategy. Policy implications may matter to federal governments as the companies in a country appear to profit from the increase in labor rights. Finally, improvements in financial markets lead to economic growth, especially in less developed markets. The findings of this study also have implications for countries with a low labor rights score – equity market enhancement should be one more reason why they might want to take further steps to strengthen labor rights.

It is important to mention that this study has several limitations, most of which are due to the paucity of data. First, political risk within the individual countries is not being considered, as publicly available risk databases only go back until 1995, which does not cover the entire sample period. It may be argued that it is not necessary to control for political risk as labor rights itself already reflect a form of political risk. Second, the annual data used in this study do not allow conclusions to be drawn on the immediate impact on equity markets. Third, lagged dependent variables could be used to trace the longer-term impact of labor reforms. Finally, the impact of labor rights on other stock market development metrics, such as the size and liquidity of the market, could also be examined.

NOTES

1. Mandelker and Rhee (1984). In their study, the authors examine the relationship between the degree of operating leverage and degree of financial leverage on the systematic risk of common stock. This is used to come up with the Mandelker and Rhee degree of operating leverage.

2. The model was run with different combinations of these controls to ensure against multicollinearity. Robustness checks were conducted and no multicollinearity was detected.

ACKNOWLEDGEMENTS AND DISCLAIMERS

This chapter is adapted from a study conducted by the author while a student in the School of Business, University at Albany. The author would like to thank the participants at the World Finance Conference, 2019, for their input.

The research in this chapter and the inferences and opinions put forth in the chapter are solely the views of the author. They do not and are not meant to represent the position or opinions of International School of Management, Germany, nor represent the official position of any of its employees or management team members.

The chapter was previously published in a similar form as a thesis, and no contract was signed that would prohibit republishing.

REFERENCES

Barnett, M. L., & Salomon, R. M. (2006). Beyond dichotomy: The curvilinear relationship between social responsibility and financial performance. *Strategic Management Journal, 27*(11), 1101–1122.

Bell, B., & Machin, S. (2018). Minimum wages and firm value. *Journal of Labor Economics, 36*(1), 159–195.

Bengoa, M., & Sanchez-Robles, B. (2003). Foreign direct investment, economic freedom and growth: New evidence from Latin America. *European Journal of Political Economy, 19*(3), 529–545.

Billmeier, A., & Massa, I. (2009). What drives stock market development in emerging markets—Institutions, remittances, or natural resources? *Emerging Markets Review, 10*(1), 23–35.

Chen, H. J., Kacperczyk, M., & Ortiz-Molina, H. (2011). Labor unions, operating flexibility, and the cost of equity. *Journal of Financial and Quantitative Analysis, 46*(1), 25–58.

Chen, N. F., Roll, R., & Ross, S. A. (1986). Economic forces and the stock market. *Journal of Business, 59*(3), 383–403.

Davies, A. C. (2004). *Perspectives on labour law*. Cambridge: Cambridge University Press.

Diermeier, J. J. (1990). Capital market expectations: The macro factors. In *Managing investment portfolios: A dynamic process* Boston: Warren, Gorham and Lamont.

Edmans, A., Li, L., & Zhang, C. (2014). *Employee satisfaction, labor market flexibility, and stock returns around the world* (No. w20300). National Bureau of Economic Research.

Fama, E. F. (1991a). Stock returns, real activity, inflation, and money. *The American Economic Review, 71*(4), 545–565.

Fama, E. F. (1991b). Efficient capital markets: II. *The Journal of Finance, 46*(5), 1575–1617.

Fama, E. F., & French, K. R. (1989). Business conditions and expected returns on stocks and bonds. *Journal of financial economics, 25*(1), 23–49.

Gwartney, J. D., Holcombe, R. G., & Lawson, R. A. (2004). Economic freedom, institutional quality, and cross-country differences in income and growth. *Cato Journal, 24*, 205.

Gwartney, J., & Lawson, R. (2003). The concept and measurement of economic freedom. *European Journal of Political Economy, 19*(3), 405–430.

Gospel, H., Pendleton, A., & Vitols, S. (Eds.). (2014). *Financialization, new investment funds, and labour: An international comparison.* Oxford: Oxford University Press.

Keim, D. B., & Stambaugh, R. F. (1986). Predicting returns in the stock and bond markets. *Journal of Financial Economics, 17*(2), 357–390.

Lawson, R. A., & Roychoudhury, S. (2008). Economic freedom and equity prices among US states. *Credit and Financial Management Review, 14*(4), 25–35.

Levine, R. (1997). Financial development and economic growth: Views and agenda. *Journal of Economic Literature, 35*(2), 688–726. Retrieved from http://www.jstor.org/stable/2729790

Li, K. (2002). What explains the growth of global equity markets. *Canadian Investment Review, 15*, 23–30.

Mandelker, G. N., & Rhee, S. G. (1984). The impact of the degrees of operating and financial leverage on systematic risk of common stock. *Journal of Financial and Quantitative Analysis, 19*(1), 45–57.

Miller, K. D., Jeffrey, F. J., & Mandelker, G. (1976). The "Fisher effect" for risky assets: An empirical investigation. *The Journal of Finance, 31*(2), 447–458.

MSCI. (2017). *Market classification.* MSCI Market Resources. https://www.msci.com/our-solutions/indexes/market-classification

Quazi, R. (2007). Economic freedom and foreign direct investment in East Asia. *Journal of the Asia Pacific Economy, 12*(3), 329–344.

Reilly, F. K., Wright, D. J., & Johnson, R. R. (2007). Analysis of the interest rate sensitivity of common stocks. *The Journal of Portfolio Management, 33*(3), 85–107.

Smimou, K., & Karabegovic, A. (2010). On the relationship between economic freedom and equity returns in the emerging markets: Evidence from the Middle East and North Africa (MENA) stock markets. *Emerging Markets Review, 11*(2), 119–151. doi:10.1016/j.ememar.2010.01.003

Stocker, M. L. (2005). Equity returns and economic freedom. *CATO Journal, 25*(3), 583–594.

Taylor, F. W. (2004). *Scientific management.* London: Routledge.

INDEX

Printed in the USA
CPSIA information can be obtained
at www.ICGtesting.com
JSHW011605070923
48022JS00005B/31